The
BRAINTEASERS
Word
Puzzles
Book

THIS IS A CARLTON BOOK

This edition published 1998 for
Parragon Book Service Ltd
Unit 13–17 Avonbridge Trading Estate,
Atlantic Road, Avonmouth
Bristol BS11 9QD

ISBN 1 75252 750 9

Printed and bound by Firmin-Didot (France)
Group Herissey
N° d'impression : 43538

The
BRAINTEASERS
Word
Puzzles
Book

SIENA

INTRODUCTION

There is every kind of word puzzle present in this book. Your word skills will be tested to the limit with anagrams, word searches, riddles, grid problems, jumbled words, word ladders, logic problems and the list goes on and on. There are over 250 word conundrums covering these pages, so they should keep you busy for quite some time.

Take this handy book anywhere with you and you can entertain yourself while exercising those brain cells and increasing your vocabulary skills. Some of these problems will involve a bit of lateral and logical thinking which should give you a good mental workout.

These are fun puzzles, some of which are on the easy side others which are more testing. No special skills are needed beyond common sense, basic literacy, and a tenacious will not to give up. So more than anything, enjoy!

WORD PUZZLE 1

Place one letter in the middle of this diagram. Four five-letter words can now be rearranged from each straight line of letters. What is the letter and what are the words?

ANSWER 62

WORD PUZZLE 2

Arrange the tiles in this diagram so that they form
a square. When this is done correctly four words
can be read down and across. What are the words?

ANSWER 10

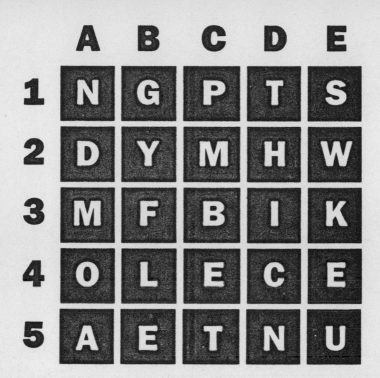

	A	B	C	D	E
1	N	G	P	T	S
2	D	Y	M	H	W
3	M	F	B	I	K
4	O	L	E	C	E
5	A	E	T	N	U

A5 C1 E3 D2 C3 E2 B4 A5 E3 B1 D3 A3 C4 D5 D1 C5

B2 D4 E1 A1 A4 B3 C2 B5 A2 B4 E4 D1 A2 E5 A4 E1

WORD PUZZLE 3

Select one of the two letters from the grid, in accordance with the reference shown, and place it in the word frame. When the correct letters have been chosen a sixteen-letter word can be read. What is the word?

ANSWER 103

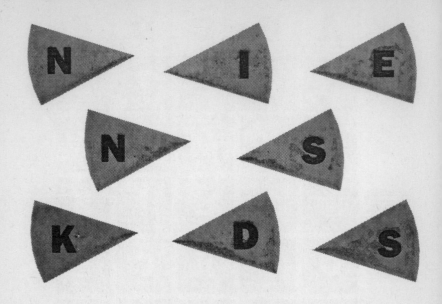

WORD PUZZLE 4

Make a circle out of these shapes.
When the correct circle has been found an English
word can be read clockwise. What is the word?

ANSWER 51

WORD PUZZLE 5

Move from circle to touching circle collecting the
letters of GOLD. Always start at the G.
How many different ways are there to do this?

ANSWER 92

BEAST	ADDER
DECOR	PILAF
HERON	PYGMY
BATON	TAXIS
HUMAN	ROUND

WORD PUZZLE 6

Six of the words in the diagram are associated for some reason. Find the words and then work out whether SHELL belongs to the group.

ANSWER 40

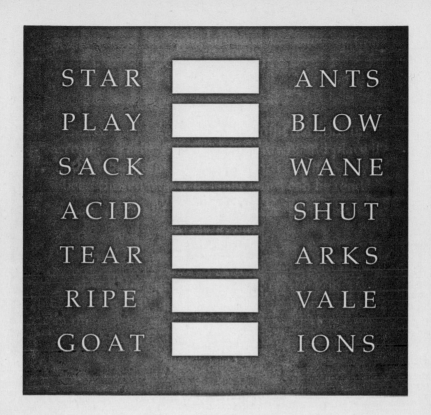

WORD PUZZLE 7

Change the second letter of each word to the left
and the right. Two other English words must be
formed. Place the letter used in the empty section.
When this has been completed for all the words
another English word can be read down.
What is the word?

ANSWER 82

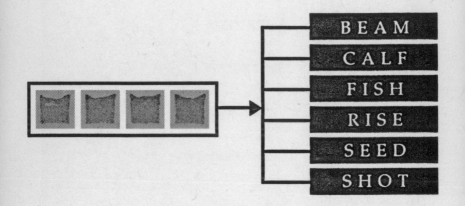

WORD PUZZLE 8

Which English word of four letters can be attached
to the front of the words shown in the diagram to
create six other words?

ANSWER 30

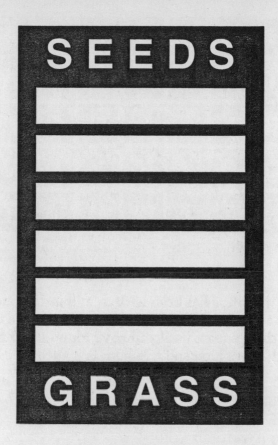

WORD PUZZLE 9

Complete the word ladder by changing one letter of each word per step. The newly created word must be found in the dictionary. What are the words to turn SEEDS to GRASS?

ANSWER 72

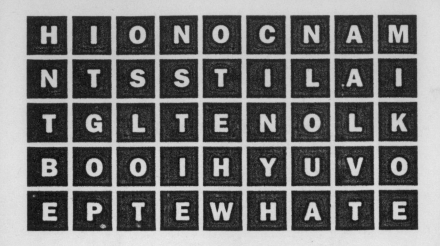

H	I	O	N	O	C	N	A	M
N	T	S	S	T	I	L	A	I
T	G	L	T	E	N	O	L	K
B	O	O	I	H	Y	U	V	O
E	P	T	E	W	H	A	T	E

WORD PUZZLE 10

A quotation has been written in this diagram.
Find the start letter and move from square to
touching square until you have found it. What is
the quotation and to whom is it attributed?

ANSWER 20

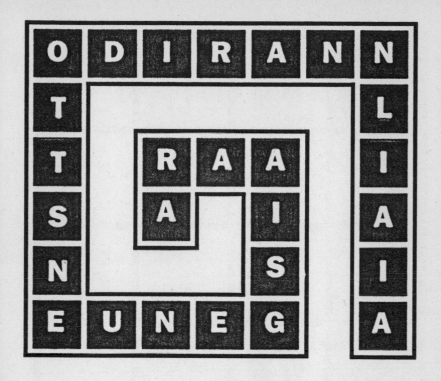

WORD PUZZLE 11

The names of three countries are to be found in the diagram. The letters of the names are in the order they normally appear. What are the countries?

ANSWER 61

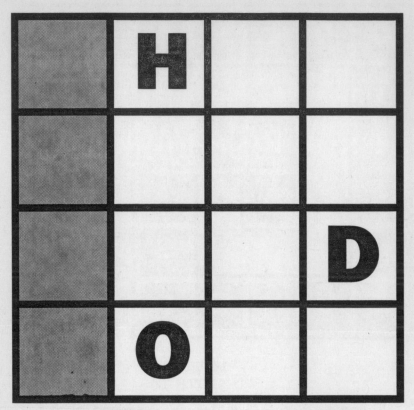

NEED   **AWAY**

DOWN   **SHOP**

WORD PUZZLE 12

If you fill the four words into the grid in the correct order, something found on the beach will be revealed in the shaded column. What is it?

ANSWER 262

Villain	B					U		

Fruit	B	U				R	

Plan				P			T

Famous pirate		L			B		R	

For growing plants		E		H			E

WORD PUZZLE 13

The clues below will help you to find words to fill the spaces. To help you even more we can tell you that the first syllable of each word could be found in a paint box.

ANSWER 233

1. **arin**

2. **usn**

3. **nsow**

4. **ahil**

WORD PUZZLE 14

When rearranged, the anagrams below will turn
into four types of weather. Can you work
out what they are?

ANSWER 219

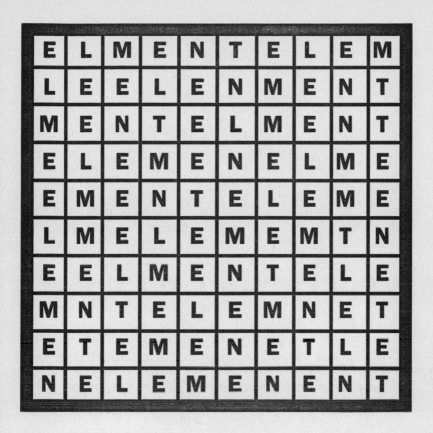

WORD PUZZLE 15

Can you find the word ELEMENT? It appears only
once in a horizontal, vertical or diagonal line.

ANSWER 207

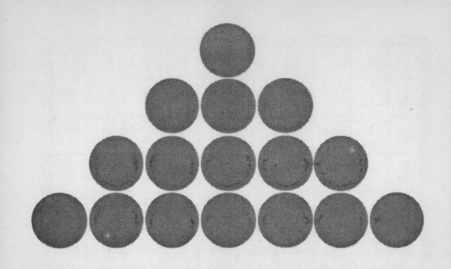

AADDIIIILLLQTUVWY

WORD PUZZLE 16

Place the letters shown into the diagram in such a way that three words can be read across and one down the middle.
What are the words?

ANSWER 9

WORD PUZZLE 17

Start at the bottom letter M and move from circle to touching circle to the N at the top right. How many different ways are there of collecting the nine letters of MANHATTAN?

ANSWER 102

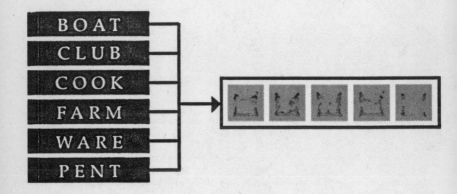

WORD PUZZLE 18

Which English word of five letters can be attached
to the back of the words shown in the diagram to
create six other words?

ANSWER 50

WORD PUZZLE 19

Select one letter from each of the segments.
When the correct letters have been found a word of
eight letters can be read clockwise.
What is the word?

ANSWER 91

1. **ram**

2. **ahed**

3. **elg**

4. **ofot**

WORD PUZZLE 20

Can you solve these anagrams to reveal four
well-known parts of the body?

ANSWER 242

FORK   **KNEE**

POLE   **OMEN**

WORD PUZZLE 21

Fill in the words in the correct order and in
the shaded column you will be able to see
something that comes out at night.

ANSWER 252

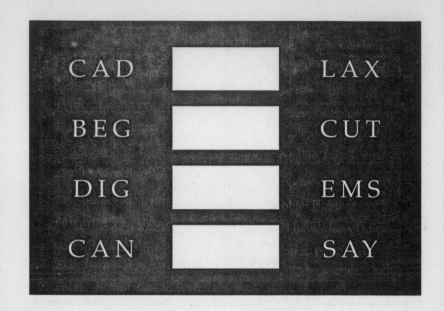

CAD		LAX
BEG		CUT
DIG		EMS
CAN		SAY

WORD PUZZLE 22

Place two letters in the empty space which, when
added to the end of the words to the left and to the
beginning of the right, form other English words.
When this is completed another word
can be read downwards. What is the word?

ANSWER 39

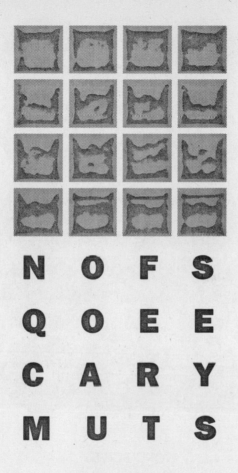

N	O	F	S
Q	O	E	E
C	A	R	Y
M	U	T	S

WORD PUZZLE 23

Take the letters and arrange them correctly in the column under which they appear. Once this has been done an historical character will appear. Who is the person?

ANSWER 81

WORD PUZZLE 24

Start at the bottom letter F and move from circle to
touching circle to the N at the top right. How many
different ways are there of collecting the nine
letters of FISHERMAN?

ANSWER 29

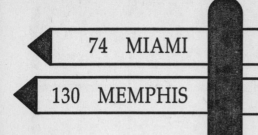

WORD PUZZLE 25

This is a meaningless signpost but there is a
twisted form of logic behind the figures. Discover
the logic and find the distance to Dallas.
How far is it?

ANSWER 71

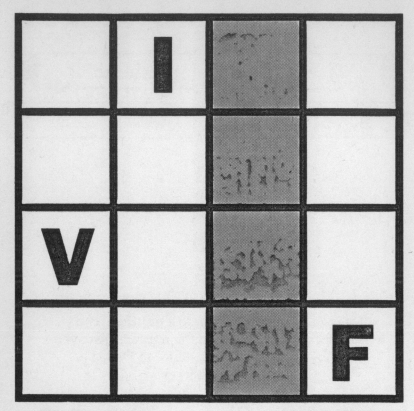

BOOK   **CHEF**

VASE   **BIRD**

WORD PUZZLE 26

If you fill in these four words correctly you will
find a type of flower in the shaded column.

ANSWER 211

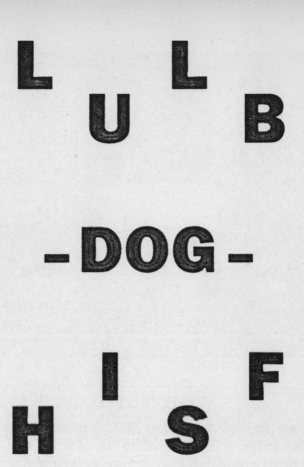

WORD PUZZLE 27

This is one strange dog! If you take the two groups
of mixed-up letters and add one to the front and
one to the end you will come up with the
seven-letter names of two very different creatures.

ANSWER 270

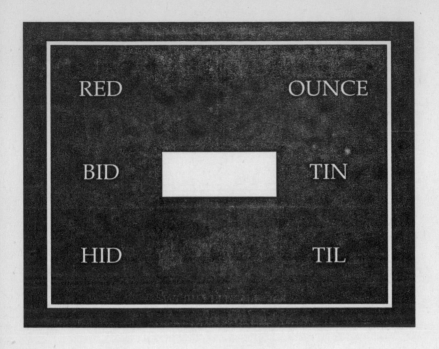

RED   OUNCE

BID   TIN

HID   TIL

WORD PUZZLE 28

Place an English word of THREE letters in the empty space. This word, when added to the end of the three words to the left and to the beginning of the three words to the right, will form six other words. What is the word?

ANSWER 19

WORD PUZZLE 29

Arrange the tiles in this diagram so that they form a square. When this is done correctly four words can be read down and across. What are the words?

ANSWER 8

WORD PUZZLE 30

Place one letter in the middle of this diagram. Four five-letter words can now be rearranged from each straight line of letters. What is the letter and what are the words?

ANSWER 60

	A	B	C	D	E
1	T	I	E	T	S
2	G	O	A	N	D
3	A	V	H	N	H
4	S	M	G	I	K
5	G	I	N	L	Y

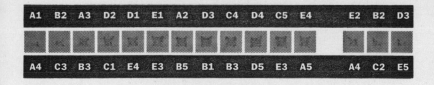

A1	B2	A3	D2	D1	E1	A2	D3	C4	D4	C5	E4		E2	B2	D3
A4	C3	B3	C1	E4	E3	B5	B1	B3	D5	E3	A5		A4	C2	E5

WORD PUZZLE 31

Select one of the two letters from the grid, in
accordance with the reference shown, and place it
in the word frame. When the correct letters have
been chosen an occasion can be read.
What is the occasion?

ANSWER 101

WORD PUZZLE 32

Make a circle out of these shapes.
When the correct circle has been found an English
word can be read clockwise. What is the word?

ANSWER 49

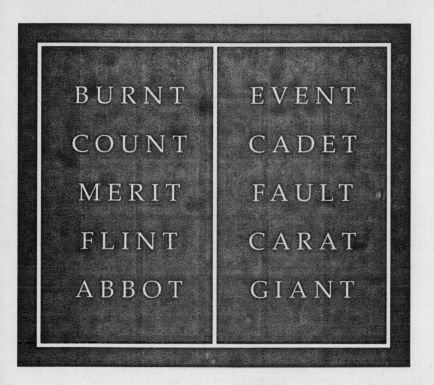

BURNT	EVENT
COUNT	CADET
MERIT	FAULT
FLINT	CARAT
ABBOT	GIANT

WORD PUZZLE 33

Five of the words in the diagram are associated for
some reason. Find the words and then work out
whether PLANT belongs to the group.

ANSWER 90

Small piece of wire driven
through sheets of paper to
hold them together . . . .

A crayon for drawing . . . .

The lightest hue . . . .

You eat off them . . . .

Folds often found in a
girl's skirt . . . .

The leaves of a flower . . . .

WORD PUZZLE 34

The answers to the six clues below are all
anagrams of each other. What are they?

ANSWER 235

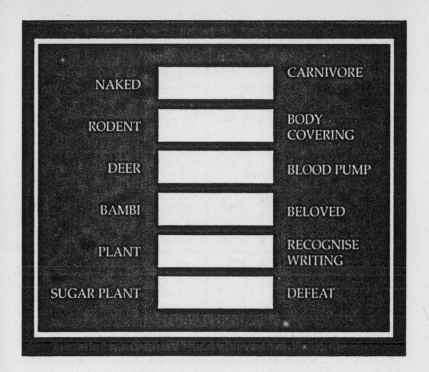

NAKED		CARNIVORE
RODENT		BODY COVERING
DEER		BLOOD PUMP
BAMBI		BELOVED
PLANT		RECOGNISE WRITING
SUGAR PLANT		DEFEAT

WORD PUZZLE 35

Each of the following sets of clues should give you a pair of homophones (words that sound the same but have different meanings).

ANSWER 273

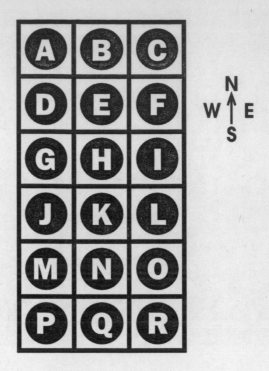

WORD PUZZLE 36

The diagram shows a plan of the secret head
quarters of the dreaded Crime Syndicate
International. By following the instructions
clearly you can reach the Boss's office and
apprehend him. Exciting, isn't it?
Start at the square two places south of the one
in the middle of the top line. Go 1 square east
and 2 south. Now go 2 squares west and 4 north.
The room you want is now 1 square SE.
Which is the final square?

ANSWER 256

	a	b	c	d	e
1	T	R	I	Y	D
2	O	L	A	G	P
3	W	E	H	N	S

1. 3D 3B 1C 2D 3C

2. 3E 3D 2A 3A 1D

3. 1B 3B 2C 1E 1D

4. 1A 3C 2A 1B 3D

5. 2B 2C 1B 2D 3B

WORD PUZZLE 37

Can you work out the five words below?

ANSWER 213

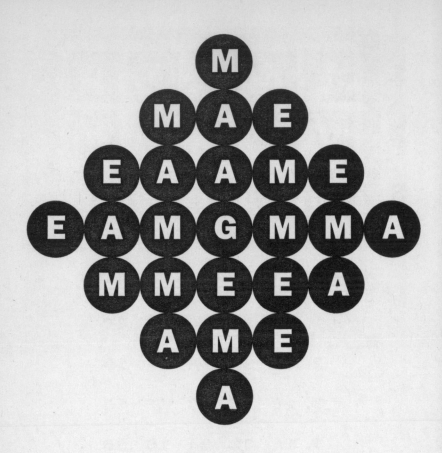

WORD PUZZLE 38

Move from circle to touching circle collecting the
letters of GAME. Always start at the G.
How many different ways are there to do this?

ANSWER 38

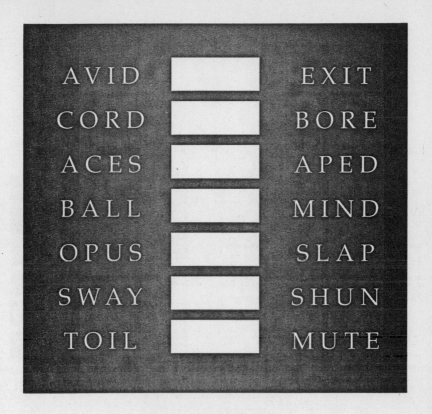

AVID   [ ]   EXIT

CORD   [ ]   BORE

ACES   [ ]   APED

BALL   [ ]   MIND

OPUS   [ ]   SLAP

SWAY   [ ]   SHUN

TOIL   [ ]   MUTE

WORD PUZZLE 39

Change the second letter of each word to the left
and the right. Two other English words must be
formed. Place the letter used in the empty section.
When this has been completed for all the words
another English word can be read down. What is
the word?

ANSWER 80

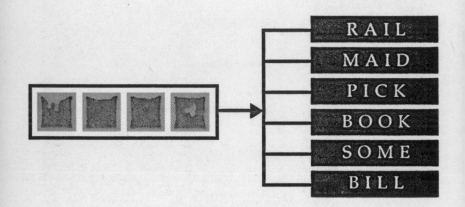

RAIL

MAID

PICK

BOOK

SOME

BILL

WORD PUZZLE 40

Which English word of four letters can be attached
to the front of the words shown in the diagram to
create six other words?

ANSWER 28

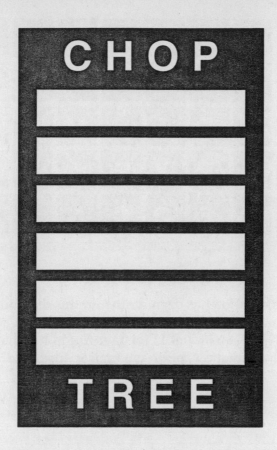

WORD PUZZLE 41

Complete the word ladder by changing one letter
of each word per step. The newly created word
must be found in the dictionary. What are the
words to turn CHOP to TREE?

ANSWER 70

WORD PUZZLE 42

A quotation has been written in this diagram. Find the start letter and move from square to touching square until you have found it. What is the quotation and to whom is it attributed?

ANSWER 18

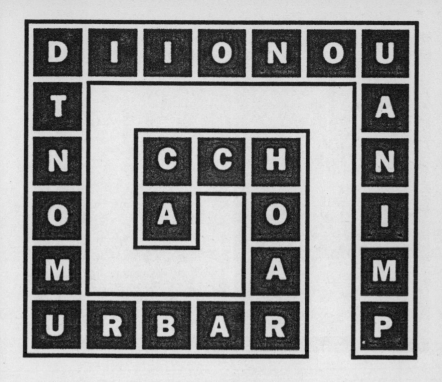

WORD PUZZLE 43

The names of four musical instruments are to be
found in the diagram. The letters of the names are
in the order they normally appear. What are the
musical instruments?

ANSWER 59

BIG	BRIAN
OLD	BEARD
UNION	NORMAN
BLUE	GLORY
GREEN	BEN
STORMIN'	JACK

WORD PUZZLE 44

The following are nicknames which have been
mixed up. Some of them belong to things and some
to people. When you have sorted them out you
should find one pair which doesn't fit.

ANSWER 238

WORD PUZZLE 45

Find the letter to place at the centre of the wheel
which will turn all the spokes into five-letter words.
Each word starts with the same letter.

ANSWER 254

AEFFFFIIIMRRRRST

WORD PUZZLE 46

Place the letters shown into the diagram in such a way that three words can be read across and one down the middle.
What are the words?

ANSWER 7

WORD PUZZLE 47

Start at the bottom letter N and move from circle to
touching circle to the E at the top right. How many
different ways are there of collecting the nine
letters of NECTARINE?

ANSWER 100

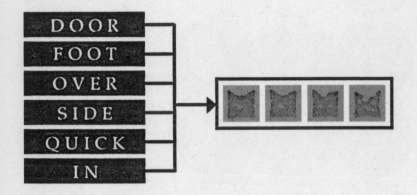

DOOR

FOOT

OVER

SIDE

QUICK

IN

WORD PUZZLE 48

Which English word of four letters can be attached
to the back of the words shown in the diagram to
create six other words?

ANSWER 48

WORD PUZZLE 49

Select one letter from each of the segments.
When the correct letters have been found a word of
eight letters can be read clockwise.
What is the word?

ANSWER 89

ACHE **WOLF**

HAIR **TAXI**

WORD PUZZLE 50

Place the words into the grid in such a way that
something hot can be seen in the shaded column.

ANSWER 208

OLIVER	WASHINGTON
MAHATMA	ROBERTS
MICHELLE	CROMWELL
GEORGE	GANDHI
ROBIN	PFEIFFER
JULIA	CODY
WILLIAM	HOOD

WORD PUZZLE 51

In Madame Twoswords' famous waxworks
Walter Foole, the newest assistant, has mixed up
the labels on the dummies. Can you sort them
out and help this dummy keep his job?

ANSWER 227

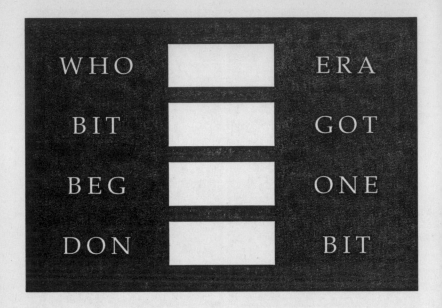

WORD PUZZLE 52

Place two letters in the empty space which, when added to the end of the words to the left and to the beginning of the right, form other English words. When this is completed another word can be read down. What is the word?

ANSWER 37

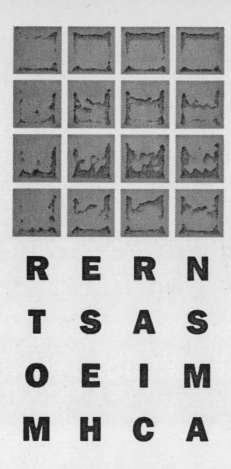

R	E	R	N
T	S	A	S
O	E	I	M
M	H	C	A

WORD PUZZLE 53

Take the letters and arrange them correctly in the column under which they appear. Once this has been done a famous person will appear.
Who is the person?

ANSWER 79

AFTER THE

DOUBLE WEDDING, THE

TWO • • • • • • WALKED

THROUGH THE HALL,

WHICH WAS LITTERED

WITH THE • • • • • •

FROM THE PARTY HELD

THE PREVIOUS NIGHT.

WORD PUZZLE 54

Two words using the same letters in their construction can be used to replace the dots in this sentence. The sentence will then make sense. Each dot is one letter. What are the words?

ANSWER 27

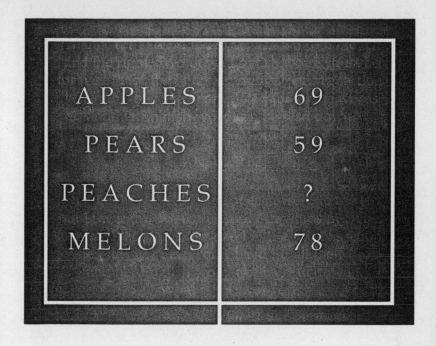

APPLES	69
PEARS	59
PEACHES	?
MELONS	78

WORD PUZZLE 55

Here are some fruit. The number of each is set
alongside the name of the fruit in the diagram.
There is a relationship between the number
and the letters of the names.
How many peaches are there?

ANSWER 69

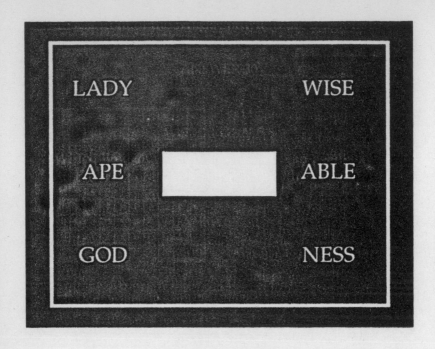

LADY   WISE

APE   ABLE

GOD   NESS

WORD PUZZLE 56

Place an English word of FOUR letters in the empty space. This word, when added to the end of the three words to the left and to the beginning of the three words to the right, will form six other words. What is the word?

ANSWER 17

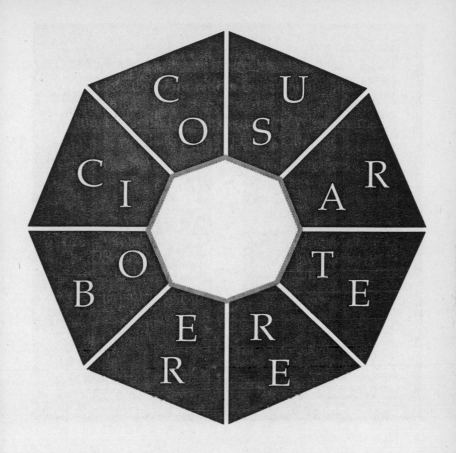

WORD PUZZLE 57

Place one letter in the middle of this diagram. Four five-letter words can now be rearranged from each straight line of letters. What is the letter and what are the words?

ANSWER 58

SAG	?	WASH
THROW	?	ARROW
FIRE	?	ARK
PRIME	?	ANGER
HER	?	LOPE
DRAM	?	VERSION
BE	?	RATE
ARE	?	BATE
FORGE	?	CUBA
PEN	?	LEDGE
YET	?	RATE

WORD PUZZLE 58

Add one letter to each line which will end the
left word and start the right word, changing
both into new English words. Reading down,
a popular star from the world of sport will
be revealed. Which one?

ANSWER 278

- - RTUG - -

- - NGA - -

- - MAN - -

- - RMA - -

- - EE - -

WORD PUZZLE 59

The following groups of letters are all names of countries from which two-letter 'heads' and 'tails' have been removed. How many can you recognise?

ANSWER 226

WORD PUZZLE 60

Arrange the tiles in this diagram so that they form a square. When this is done correctly four words can be read downwards and across.
What are the words?

ANSWER 6

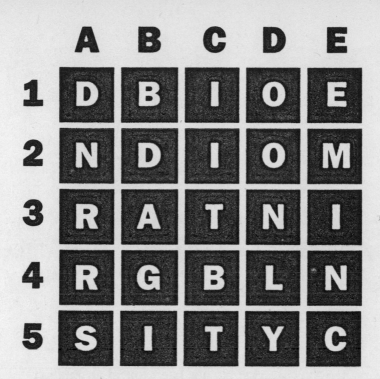

	A	B	C	D	E
1	D	B	I	O	E
2	N	D	I	O	M
3	R	A	T	N	I
4	R	G	B	L	N
5	S	I	T	Y	C

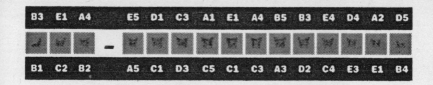

| B3 | E1 | A4 | | E5 | D1 | C3 | A1 | E1 | A4 | B5 | B3 | E4 | D4 | A2 | D5 |
| B1 | C2 | B2 | | A5 | C1 | D3 | C5 | C1 | C3 | A3 | D2 | C4 | E3 | E1 | B4 |

WORD PUZZLE 61

Select one of the two letters from the grid, in
accordance with the reference shown, and place it
in the word frame. When the correct letters have
been chosen a (hyphenated) word can be read.
What is the word?

ANSWER 99

WORD PUZZLE 62

Make a circle out of these shapes.
When the correct circle has been found an English
word can be read clockwise. What is the word?

ANSWER 47

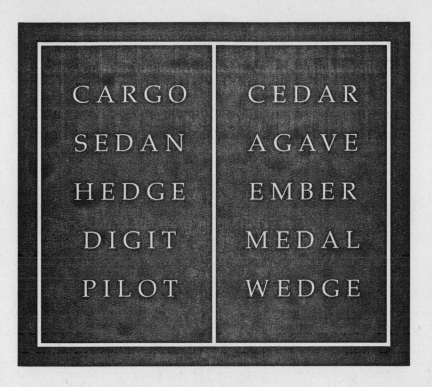

CARGO	CEDAR
SEDAN	AGAVE
HEDGE	EMBER
DIGIT	MEDAL
PILOT	WEDGE

WORD PUZZLE 63

Five of the words in the diagram are associated for some reason. Find the words and then work out whether SYRUP belongs to the group.

ANSWER 88

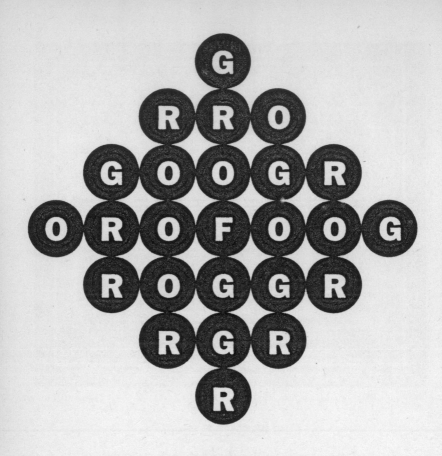

WORD PUZZLE 64

Move from circle to touching circle collecting the
letters of FROG. Always start at the F.
How many different ways are there to do this?

ANSWER 36

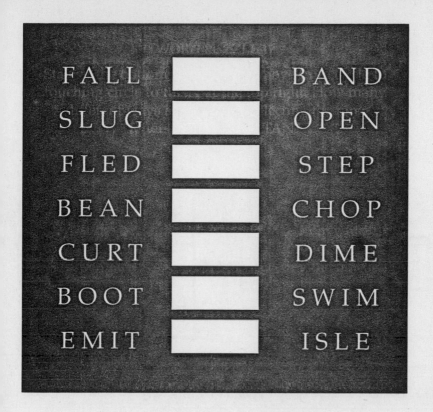

FALL		BAND
SLUG		OPEN
FLED		STEP
BEAN		CHOP
CURT		DIME
BOOT		SWIM
EMIT		ISLE

WORD PUZZLE 65

Change the second letter of each word to the left
and the right. Two other English words must be
formed. Place the letter used in the empty section.
When this has been completed for all the words
another English word can be read down.
What is the word?

ANSWER 78

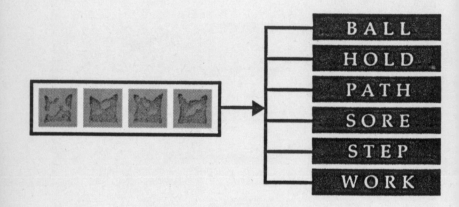

WORD PUZZLE 66

Which English word of four letters can be attached
to the front of the words shown in the diagram to
create six other words?

ANSWER 26

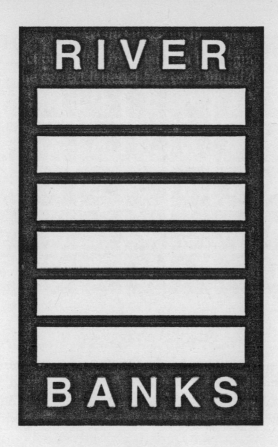

WORD PUZZLE 67

Complete the word ladder by changing one letter
of each word per step. The newly created word
must be found in the dictionary. What are the
words to turn RIVER to BANKS?

ANSWER 68

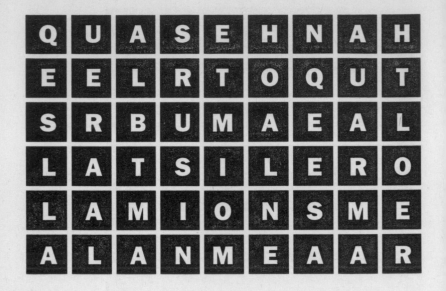

Q	U	A	S	E	H	N	A	H
E	E	L	R	T	O	Q	U	T
S	R	B	U	M	A	E	A	L
L	A	T	S	I	L	E	R	O
L	A	M	I	O	N	S	M	E
A	L	A	N	M	E	A	A	R

WORD PUZZLE 68

A quotation has been written in this diagram.
Find the start letter and move from square to
touching square until you have found it. What is
the quotation and to whom is it attributed?

ANSWER 16

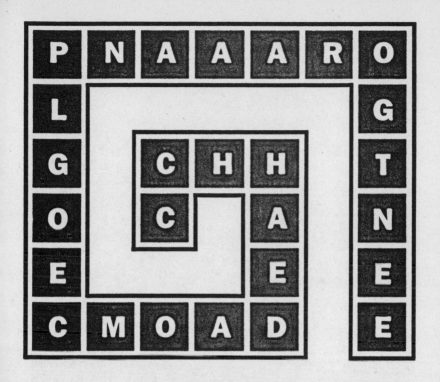

WORD PUZZLE 69

The names of three drinks are to be found in the
diagram. The letters of the names are in the order
they normally appear. What are the drinks?

ANSWER 57

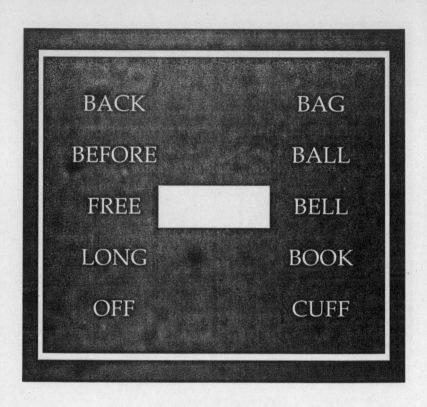

BACK	BAG
BEFORE	BALL
FREE	BELL
LONG	BOOK
OFF	CUFF

WORD PUZZLE 70

Find a four-letter word which can be added to
the end of the words of the left-hand column
and the beginning of the words in the right-hand
column to give 10 new words.

ANSWER 209

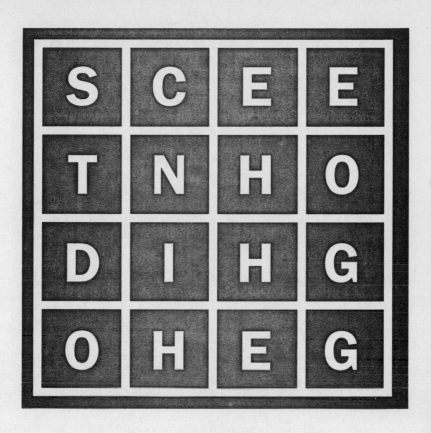

WORD PUZZLE 71

Re-arrange the letters in the grid to find the
name of a computer game hero.

ANSWER 243

T	A	B	E	A	R	G	S	G	A
P	C	O	D	F	O	T	S	H	B
A	G	O	T	R	Q	U	N	V	D
R	T	H	F	L	M	N	A	W	R
R	C	I	D	E	S	A	K	K	A
O	R	S	G	T	U	N	E	L	P
T	A	V	T	E	C	B	O	P	O
U	G	Z	Q	S	R	L	J	R	E
H	I	Y	E	K	N	O	M	E	L
C	E	L	E	P	H	A	N	T	D

WORD PUZZLE 72

Identify the animals and fish concealed
among the letters. The words may run in
any direction and may overlap.

ANSWER 250

	pie
	conquest
	singer
	watchman
	fever
	Twain
	poppy
	duckling
	spray

WORD PUZZLE 73

Find a word or name that goes with the one we
have given and then read down the first letter of
each answer. You should find a nameless word!

ANSWER 279

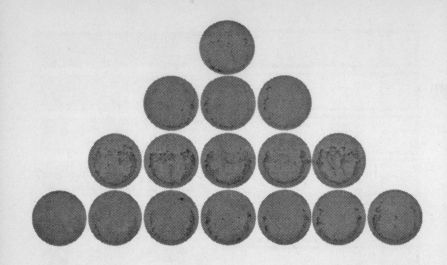

A B C E E E E E G I M O R S V Y

WORD PUZZLE 74

Place the letters shown into the diagram in such a way that three words can be read across and one down the middle. What are the words?

ANSWER 5

WORD PUZZLE 75

Start at the letter L and move from circle to touching circle to the H at the top right. How many different ways are there of collecting the nine letters of LABYRINTH?

ANSWER 98

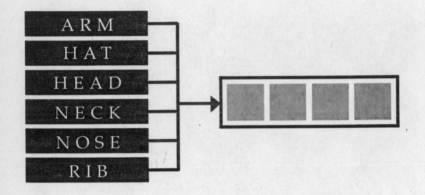

WORD PUZZLE 76

Which English word of four letters can be attached to the back of the words shown in the diagram to create six other words?

ANSWER 46

WORD PUZZLE 77

Select one letter from each of the segments.
When the correct letters have been found a word of
eight letters can be read clockwise.
What is the word?

ANSWER 87

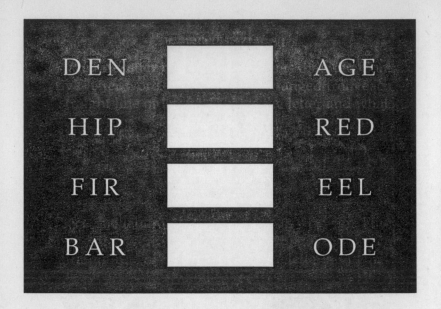

WORD PUZZLE 78

Place two letters in the empty space which, when added to the end of the words to the left and to the beginning of the right, form other English words. When this is completed another word can be read downwards. What is the word?

ANSWER 35

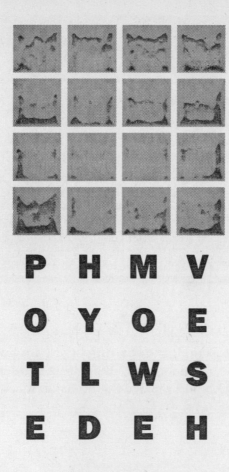

P H M V

O Y O E

T L W S

E D E H

WORD PUZZLE 79

Take the letters and arrange them correctly in the
column under which they appear.
Once this has been done a movie title will appear.
What is the movie?

ANSWER 77

AUSTRALIA	960
MADAGASCAR	1152
IRELAND	576
CUBA	?

WORD PUZZLE 80

The distances on this departure board are fictitious.
They bear a relationship to the letters in the names,
What should replace the question mark ?

ANSWER 25

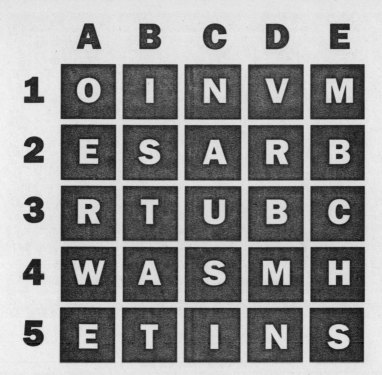

	A	B	C	D	E
1	O	I	N	V	M
2	E	S	A	R	B
3	R	T	U	B	C
4	W	A	S	M	H
5	E	T	I	N	S

B2	B1	D4	D5	A2	A3		B2	C2	D3	B4	B5	B3	A1	E5	C4
A4	C3	C1	E1	A5	D4		D1	C2	E3	E2	C2	C5	E4	D5	A1

WORD PUZZLE 81

Select one of the two letters from the grid, in accordance with the reference shown, and place it in the word frame. When the correct letters have been chosen two linked words can be read. What are the words?

ANSWER 67

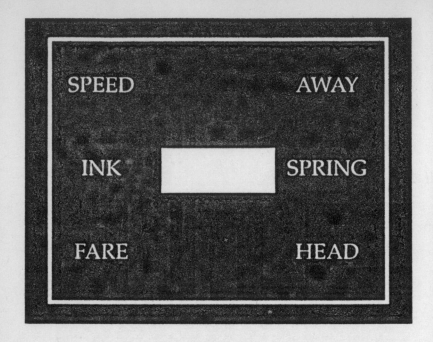

SPEED   AWAY

INK   SPRING

FARE   HEAD

WORD PUZZLE 82

Place an English word of FOUR letters in the empty space. This word, when added to the end of the three words to the left and to the beginning of the three words to the right, will form six other words. What is the word?

ANSWER 15

WORD PUZZLE 83

Place one letter in the middle of this diagram.
Four five-letter words can now be rearranged from
each straight line of letters. What is the letter and
what are the words?

ANSWER 56

WORD PUZZLE 84

Arrange the tiles in this diagram so that they form
a square. When this is done correctly four words
can be read down and across. What are the words?

ANSWER 4

	A	B	C	D	E
1	Z	E	E	N	A
2	A	A	C	H	T
3	I	S	T	I	R
4	C	L	C	R	U
5	P	I	O	I	Y

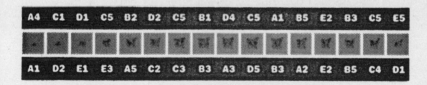

| A4 | C1 | D1 | C5 | B2 | D2 | C5 | B1 | D4 | C5 | A1 | B5 | E2 | B3 | C5 | E5 |

| A1 | D2 | E1 | E3 | A5 | C2 | C3 | B3 | A3 | D5 | B3 | A2 | E2 | B5 | C4 | D1 |

WORD PUZZLE 85

Select one of the two letters from the grid, in
accordance with the reference shown, and place it
in the word frame. When the correct letters have
been chosen a sixteen-letter word can be read.
What is the word?

ANSWER 97

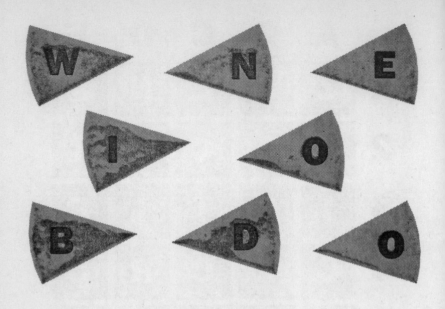

WORD PUZZLE 86

Make a circle out of these shapes.
When the correct circle has been found an English
word can be read clockwise. What is the word?

ANSWER 45

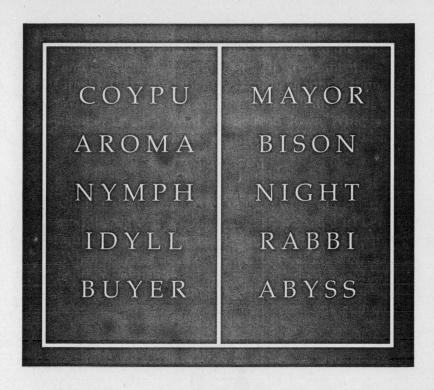

COYPU	MAYOR
AROMA	BISON
NYMPH	NIGHT
IDYLL	RABBI
BUYER	ABYSS

WORD PUZZLE 87

Five of the words in the diagram are associated for some reason. Find the words and then work out whether STYLE belongs to the group.

ANSWER 86

WORD PUZZLE 88

Move from circle to touching circle collecting the
letters of BELL. Always start at the B.
How many different ways are there to do this?

ANSWER 34

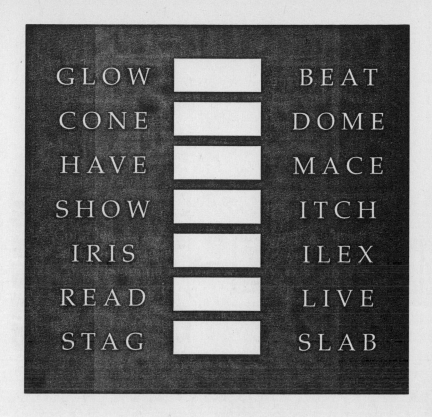

WORD PUZZLE 89

Change the second letter of each word to the left
and the right. Two other English words must be
formed. Place the letter used in the empty section.
When this has been completed for all the words
another English word can be read down.
What is the word?

ANSWER 76

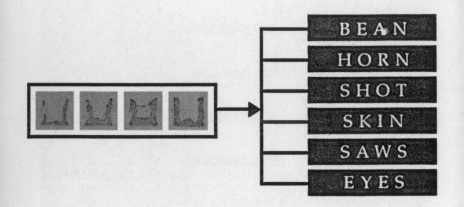

BEAN

HORN

SHOT

SKIN

SAWS

EYES

WORD PUZZLE 90

Which English word of four letters can be attached
to the front of the words shown in the diagram to
create six other words?

ANSWER 24

WORD PUZZLE 91

Complete the word ladder by changing one letter
of each word per step. The newly created word
must be found in the dictionary. What are the
words to turn PONY to CART?

ANSWER 66

BEETLE	HERE	PEPPER
CEMETERY	JESTER	REFEREE
CLEVER	KESTREL	REFERENCE
CRESCENT	LETTER	SEETHE
DETERGENT	MEDLEY	THEME
EFFECT	MESSENGER	TEPEE
ENTENTE	MERGE	VESSEL
FERMENT	METHYLENE	WHEREVER
GREENERY	NEEDLE	YEN
HELMET	NETTLES	

WORD PUZZLE 92

Below you'll find a list of words containing 'E' as their only vowel. Can you locate them in the big 'E' shape? Which is the word that appears twice?

ANSWER 274

```
M Y R E F E R E N C E N R Y R R K E
E E N V E S E R E V E R E H W W E S
S N E C E F F E C T Y M T E S S S E
Y T E E G E R F L S E E T E N N R S
R S D N R K E R E H S F E D B B N P
E E L S E R J E T E F E L T H H Y E
N J E S M R E
E H T E E S Y
E E N T J E T B Y F L E C H T E K R
R T P N Y E E R F E S E L T T E N E
G R E E T P M T E P L G E N E R E P
F R E G N E S S E M R D V E V C F P
E V T R E T L E T E M L E E H R F E
E E N E C P R R R E M S E R L M Y R P
L Y K T S P E
C R R E E K H
V E E D R E C E B E V G Y F E E R I
E T T F C S E E N E L Y H T E M H E
T E S S E T F L S M E T S E C S E M
E M E E F R F S T E S T E M L E H E
N E J R B E E T R E F E L X J V E H
T C E C R L M E T N E T N E E N E T
```

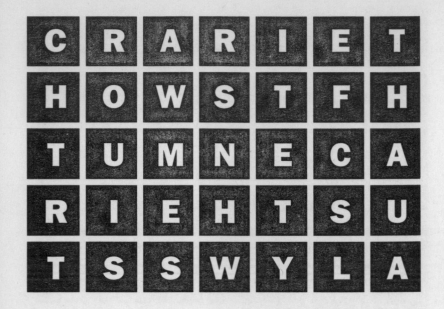

WORD PUZZLE 93

A quotation has been written in this diagram.
Find the start letter and move from square to
touching square until you have found it. What is
the quotation and to whom is it attributed?

ANSWER 14

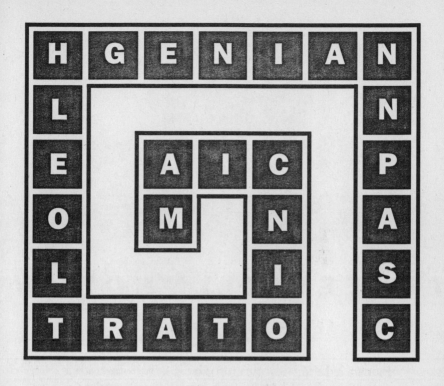

WORD PUZZLE 94

The names of three foods are to be found in the diagram. The letters of the names are in the order they normally appear. What are the foods?

ANSWER 55

A B D E E E J K L L M N O T W W

WORD PUZZLE 95

Place the letters shown into the diagram in such a
way that three words can be read across and one
down the middle. What are the words?

ANSWER 3

WORD PUZZLE 96

Start at the letter B and move from circle to touching circle to the A at the top right. How many different ways are there of collecting the nine letters of BALLERINA?

ANSWER 96

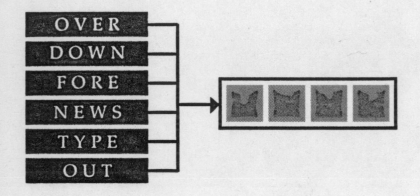

OVER
DOWN
FORE
NEWS
TYPE
OUT

WORD PUZZLE 97

Which English word of four letters can be attached
to the back of the words shown in the diagram to
create six other words?

ANSWER 44

WORD PUZZLE 98

Select one letter from each of the segments.
When the correct letters have been found a word of
eight letters can be read clockwise.
What is the word?

ANSWER 85

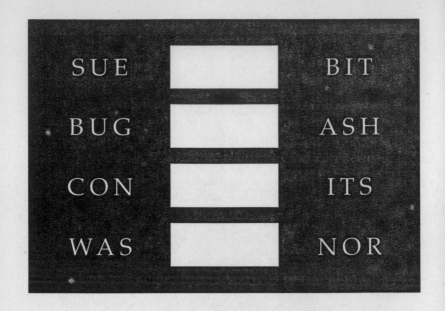

WORD PUZZLE 99

Place two letters in the empty space which, when
added to the end of the words to the left and to the
beginning of the right, form other English words.
When this is completed another word
can be read down. What is the word?

ANSWER 33

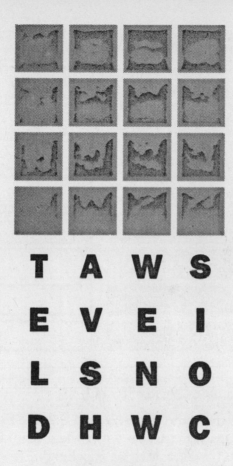

T A W S

E V E I

L S N O

D H W C

WORD PUZZLE 100

Take the letters and arrange them correctly in the column under which they appear. Once this has been done a movie title will appear. What is the movie?

ANSWER 75

Natural force	
Greater in length	
Live coal	
British sport	
Medicine in pill form	
Herb with girl's name	
Herb found in pizza	
Walk slowly	
Never-ending	

WORD PUZZLE 101

Solve the clues and you will find that the first letter
of the answers make a word when read down.
Clue: May be shocking.

ANSWER 228

1. Not slow.

2. A particular piece of ground.

3. In a tennis match there are a maximum of five.

4. A piece of work to be done.

WORD PUZZLE 102

When you solve these clues and fill the answers into the grid you will find that it reads the same down and across.

ANSWER 258

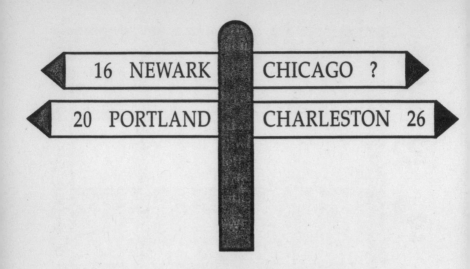

| 16 | NEWARK | CHICAGO | ? |
| 20 | PORTLAND | CHARLESTON | 26 |

WORD PUZZLE 103

This is a meaningless signpost but there is a
twisted form of logic behind the figures. Discover
the logic and find the distance to Chicago.
How far is it?

ANSWER 65

A2	B1	A1	A3	D5	E5	D2	C1	B5	A5	A4	D3	E1	B4	E1	D4
C4	A5	C4	B3	B2	B1	E1	E2	D1	D5	C5	C2	C3	E3	D2	E4

WORD PUZZLE 104

Select one of the two letters from the grid, in accordance with the reference shown, and place it in the word frame. When the correct letters have been chosen a sixteen-letter word can be read. What is the word?

ANSWER 23

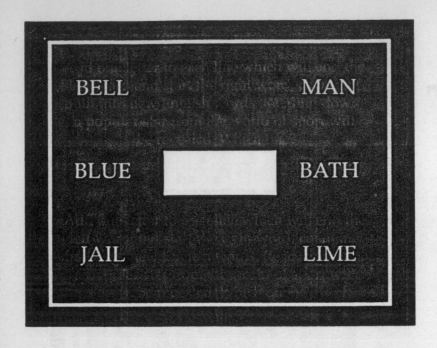

WORD PUZZLE 105

Place an English word of FOUR letters in the empty space. This word, when added to the end of the three words to the left and to the beginning of the three words to the right, will form six other words. What is the word?

ANSWER 13

WORD PUZZLE 106

Place one letter in the middle of this diagram. Four
five-letter words can now be rearranged from each
straight line of letters. What is the letter and what
are the words?

ANSWER 54

WORD PUZZLE 107

Arrange the tiles in this diagram so that they form a square. When this is done correctly four words can be read down and across. What are the words?

ANSWER 2

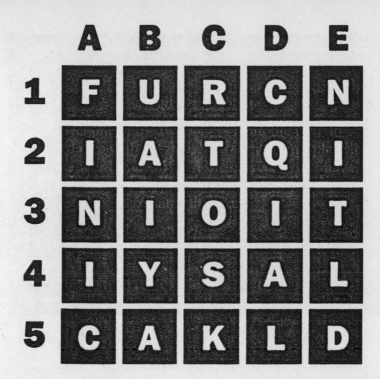

	A	B	C	D	E
1	F	U	R	C	N
2	I	A	T	Q	I
3	N	I	O	I	T
4	I	Y	S	A	L
5	C	A	K	L	D

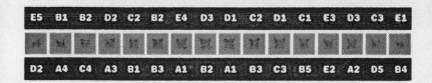

E5	B1	B2	D2	C2	B2	E4	D3	D1	C2	D1	C1	E3	D3	C3	E1

D2	A4	C4	A3	B1	B3	A1	B2	A1	B3	C3	B5	E2	A2	D5	B4

WORD PUZZLE 108

Select one of the two letters from the grid, in
accordance with the reference shown, and place it
in the word frame. When the correct letters have
been chosen a sixteen-letter word can be read.
What is the word?

ANSWER 95

JOHN	ARMSTRONG
BONHAM-CARTER	EINSTEIN
ALBERT	NEIL
TAYLOR	BONAPARTE
HELENA	RICHARD
LENNON	GERE
ELIZABETH	NAPOLEON

WORD PUZZLE 109

It is now Walter's second day working at the world renowned waxworks of Madame Twoswords and he's gone and mixed up the first names and surnames of the models. Having sorted the labels into equal piles, can you help put them in the right order before Madame has poor Walter coated in wax and put on display.

ANSWER 275

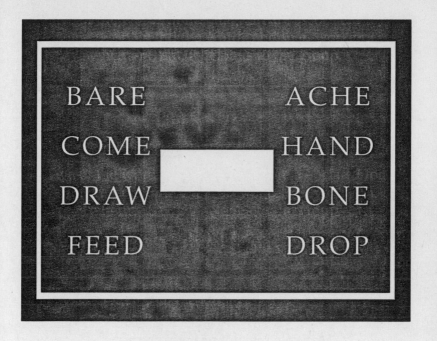

BARE		ACHE
COME		HAND
DRAW		BONE
FEED		DROP

WORD PUZZLE 110

Put a word in the middle space which makes,
when added to the end of the words on the left
and the beginning of the words on the right,
eight new eight-letter words.

ANSWER 263

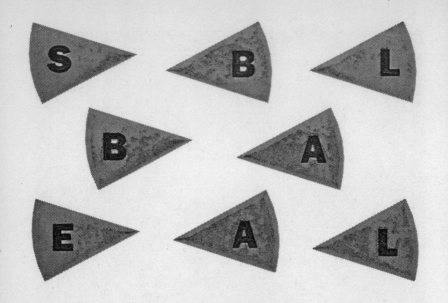

WORD PUZZLE 111

Make a circle out of these shapes.
When the correct circle has been found an English
word can be read clockwise. What is the word?

ANSWER 43

WORD PUZZLE 112

Move from circle to touching circle collecting the
letters of SILK. Always start at the S.
How many different ways are there to do this?

ANSWER 84

EPOCH	TULIP
SWINE	EXILE
OKAPI	ABBEY
DECOY	HIPPO
STEAM	BLOND

WORD PUZZLE 113

Five of the words in the diagram are associated for some reason. Find the words and then work out whether FLUTE belongs to the group.

ANSWER 32

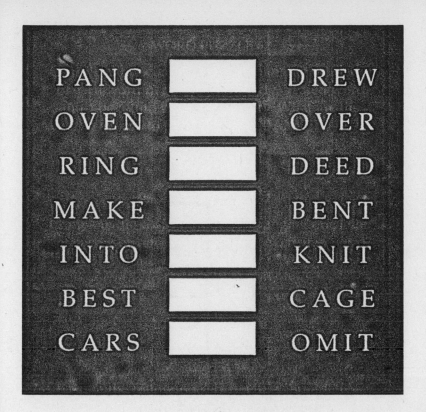

PANG ☐ DREW
OVEN ☐ OVER
RING ☐ DEED
MAKE ☐ BENT
INTO ☐ KNIT
BEST ☐ CAGE
CARS ☐ OMIT

WORD PUZZLE 114

Change the first letter of each word to the left and
the right. Two other English words must be
formed. Place the letter used in the empty section.
When this has been completed for all the words
another English word can be read downwards.
What is the word?

ANSWER 74

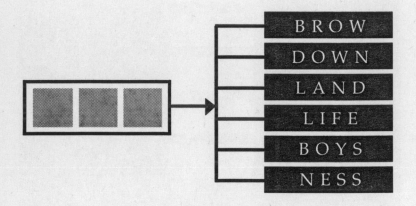

WORD PUZZLE 115

Which English word of three letters can be attached to the front of the words shown in the diagram to create six other words?

ANSWER 22

WORD PUZZLE 116

Complete the word ladder by changing one letter
of each word per step. The newly created word
must be found in the dictionary. What are the
words to turn LION to PUMA?

ANSWER 64

Violet		
Quantity		
Agreement		
Athletic competition		
Sub-continent		
Adhesive		
Wet weather gear		
Pachyderm		

WORD PUZZLE 117

When you have solved all the clues, read the first letter of the answers and you will find a hidden word. The clue is a mystery.

ANSWER 249

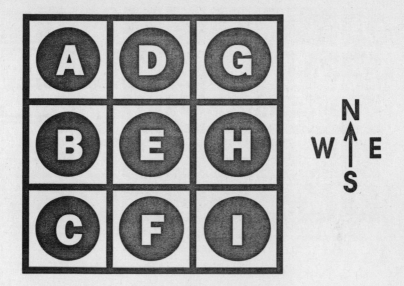

The final square is to the south of the square two places east of the square which is one place due south of the square at the extreme north west.

WORD PUZZLE 118

The diagram shows the front of a very clever type of safe. Turn each wheel in the order given and you will be able to open the door. What is the proper order?

ANSWER 210

WORD PUZZLE 119

A quotation has been written in this diagram.
Find the start letter and move from square to
touching square until you have found it. What is
the quotation and to whom is it attributed?

ANSWER 12

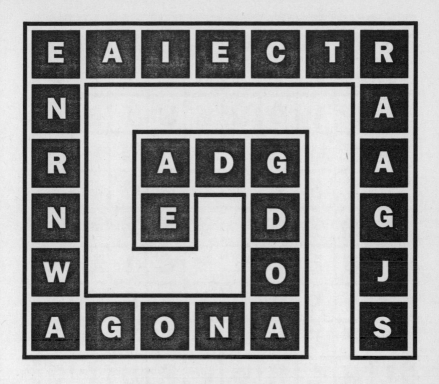

WORD PUZZLE 120

The names of three trees are to be found in the
diagram. The letters of the names are in the order
they normally appear. What are the trees?

ANSWER 53

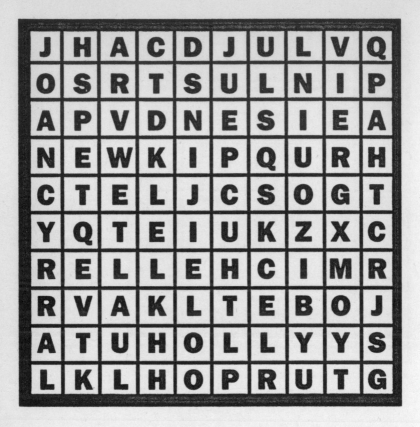

J	H	A	C	D	J	U	L	V	Q
O	S	R	T	S	U	L	N	I	P
A	P	V	D	N	E	S	I	E	A
N	E	W	K	I	P	Q	U	R	H
C	T	E	L	J	C	S	O	G	T
Y	Q	T	E	I	U	K	Z	X	C
R	E	L	L	E	H	C	I	M	R
R	V	A	K	L	T	E	B	O	J
A	T	U	H	O	L	L	Y	Y	S
L	K	L	H	O	P	R	U	T	G

WORD PUZZLE 121

Eight kids are hiding in the grid below hoping to
avoid school. Their names are: PETE, SUSIE, DICK,
MICHELLE, JOSH, HOLLY, LARRY, and JULIA.
Can you find them? The names may be spelt in any
direction, not necessarily in a straight line.

ANSWER 266

Instrument for giving commands		
Assault		
Fighting vehicle		
Strategy		
Not yet a captain		
Foe		

Clue: Part of a war

WORD PUZZLE 122

When you have solved the clues you will find
that the first letter of the answers will give a
hidden word reading down.

ANSWER 229

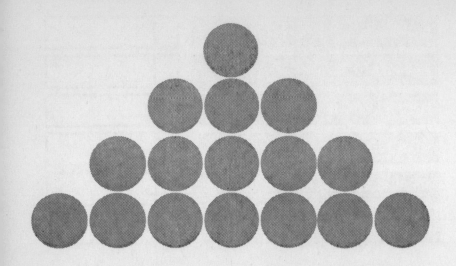

CDEHMNOOOOPPRSST

WORD PUZZLE 123

Place the letters shown into the diagram in such a way that three words can be read across and one down the middle. What are the words?

ANSWER 1

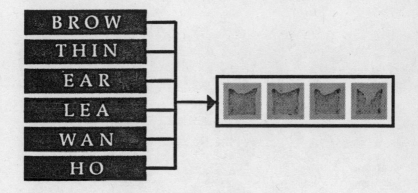

Which English word of four letters can be attached
to the back of the words shown in the diagram to
create six other words?

ANSWER 42

WORD PUZZLE 125

Start at the bottom letter A and move from circle to touching circle to the E at the top right. How many different ways are there of collecting the nine letters of ABORIGINE?

ANSWER 94

WORD PUZZLE 126

Select one letter from each of the segments.
When the correct letters have been found a word of
eight letters can be read clockwise.
What is the word?

ANSWER 83

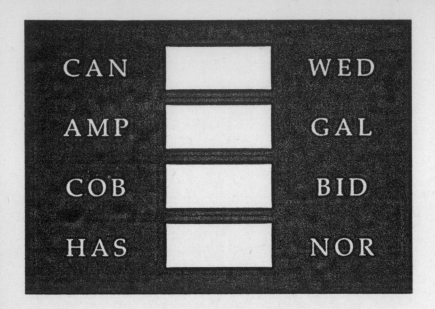

WORD PUZZLE 127

Place two letters in the empty space which, when added to the end of the words to the left and to the beginning of the right, form other English words. When this is completed another word can be read down. What is the word?

ANSWER 31

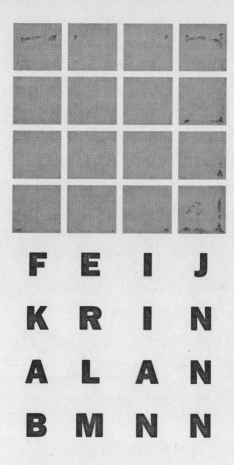

F E I J

K R I N

A L A N

B M N N

WORD PUZZLE 128

Take the letters and arrange them correctly in the
column under which they appear. Once this has
been done a famous person will appear.
Who is the person?

ANSWER 73

EIGHT TENDRIL IDOL ROD

?

WORD PUZZLE 129

This fairy tale character became confused
after failing to recognise her grandmother.
Can you sort her out?

ANSWER 212

1. To turn about on a axis

| | O | | A | | E | |

2. Juicy

| | U | | | U | | E | | |

3. Helps after dinner

| | I | | | | A | | | E | |

4. Unfriendly

| | O | | | I | | E | |

5. Of the night

| | O | | | U | | | A | |

6. A border between two countries

| | | | O | | | I | E |

7. To tear roughly

| | A | | E | | A | | E |

8. To unroll a flag

| U | | | U | | |

9. To have an unjust opinion of

| | I | | | U | | E |

10. Four times a year

| | U | A | | | E | | | |

WORD PUZZLE 130

Below are ten clues. To help you solve them, we've supplied the vowels for each answer.

ANSWER 225

THE PROFESSIONAL WRESTLER WAS OF • • • • • • BUILD AND BORE A • • • • • • AGAINST HIS OPPONENT.

WORD PUZZLE 131

Two words using the same letters in their construction can be used to replace the dots in this sentence. The sentence will then make sense. Each dot is one letter. What are the words?

ANSWER 21

16 LONDON — YORK 11

23 LIVERPOOL — BIRMINGHAM ?

WORD PUZZLE 132

The distances on this signpost are fictitious. They
bear a relationship to the letters in the names.
What should replace the question mark?

ANSWER 63

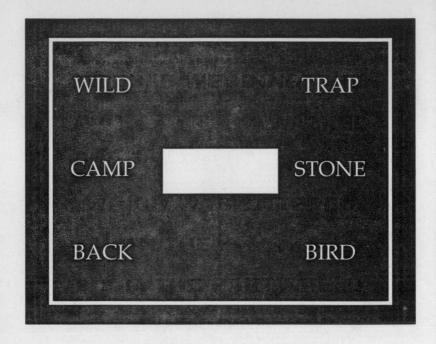

WILD   TRAP

CAMP   [   ]   STONE

BACK   BIRD

WORD PUZZLE 133

Place an English word of FOUR letters in the empty space. This word, when added to the end of the three words to the left and to the beginning of the three words to the right, will form six other words. What is the word?

ANSWER 11

WORD PUZZLE 134

Place one letter in the middle of this diagram. Four five-letter words can now be rearranged from each straight line of letters. What is the letter and what are the words?

ANSWER 52

WORD PUZZLE 135

Arrange the tiles in this diagram so that they form
a square. When this is done correctly five words
can be read downwards and across.
What are the words?

ANSWER 104

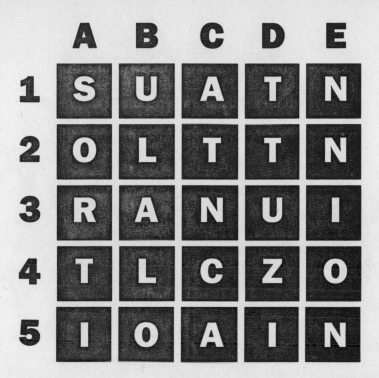

	A	B	C	D	E
1	S	U	A	T	N
2	O	L	T	T	N
3	R	A	N	U	I
4	T	L	C	Z	O
5	I	O	A	I	N

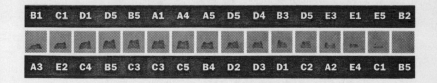

B1	C1	D1	D5	B5	A1	A4	A5	D5	D4	B3	D5	E3	E1	E5	B2
A3	E2	C4	B5	C3	C3	C5	B4	D2	D3	D1	C2	A2	E4	C1	B5

WORD PUZZLE 136

Select one of the two letters from the grid, in accordance with the reference shown, and place it in the word frame. When the correct letters have been chosen a sixteen-letter word can be read. What is the word?

ANSWER 93

WORD PUZZLE 137

Try to find out the name of this fairy tale
character. Come to think of it, that was the
point of the story!

ANSWER 260

1. TH WZRD F Z

2. CLS NCNTRS F TH THRD KND

3. PLLYNN

4. BCK T TH FTR

5. NTNL VLVT

6. BTMN RTRNS

7. BTY ND TH BST

8. HNY   SHRNK TH KDS

9. TH SND F MSC

10. JRSSC PRK

WORD PUZZLE 138

These film titles are written without vowels.
Your task is to find the missing vowels and
reveal the film.

ANSWER 253

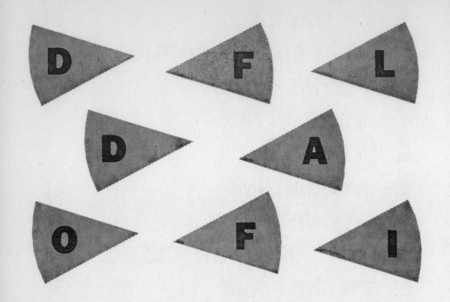

WORD PUZZLE 139

Make a circle out of these shapes.
When the correct circle has been found an English
word can be read clockwise. What is the word?

ANSWER 41

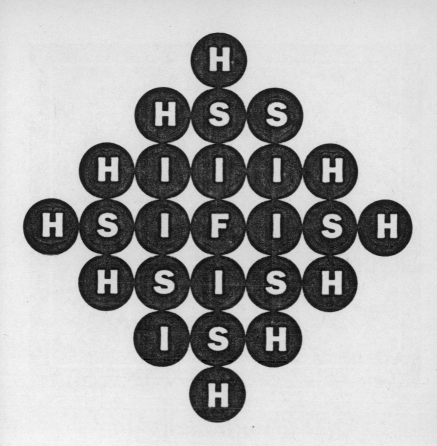

WORD PUZZLE 140

Move from circle to touching circle collecting the
letters of FISH. Always start at the F.
How many different ways are there to do this?

ANSWER 167

ASPIC	IMAGE
STEEL	ANNOY
LEAFY	COMMA
JETTY	AGENT
BEACH	CADDY

WORD PUZZLE 141

Five of the words in the diagram are associated for some reason. Find the words and then work out whether CHEER belongs to the group.

ANSWER 115

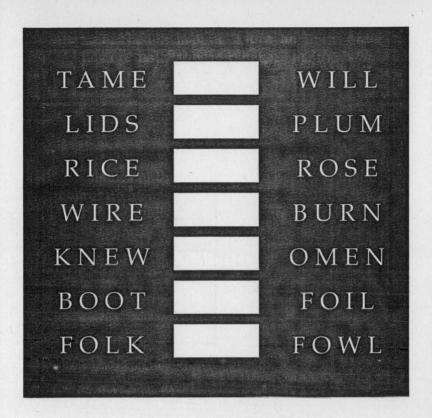

TAME		WILL
LIDS		PLUM
RICE		ROSE
WIRE		BURN
KNEW		OMEN
BOOT		FOIL
FOLK		FOWL

WORD PUZZLE 142

Change the first letter of each word to the left and
the right. Two other English words must be
formed. Place the letter used in the empty section.
When this has been completed for all the words
another English word can be read down.
What is the word?

ANSWER 134

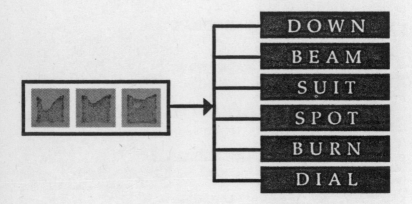

WORD PUZZLE 143

Which English word of three letters can be attached
to the front of the words shown in the diagram to
create six other words?

ANSWER 156

WORD PUZZLE 144

Complete the word ladder by changing one letter of each word per step. The newly created word must be found in the dictionary. What are the words to turn BLAZE to GLORY?

ANSWER 197

T	A	R	K	A
S	E	A	A	R
O	F	O	I	D
L	T	S	R	E
E	H	S	E	R

WORD PUZZLE 145

By moving one square up, down, right or left –
not diagonally – follow the trail of letters in
the grid and you will find the title of a
Steven Spielberg film. But beware, there
are six dummy letters included.

ANSWER 214

WORD PUZZLE 146

This kid stayed out late and lost her footing.
Can you unscramble her and give the
tale a happy ending?

ANSWER 230

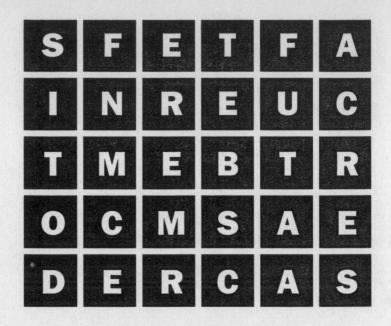

S	F	E	T	F	A
I	N	R	E	U	C
T	M	E	B	T	R
O	C	M	S	A	E
D	E	R	C	A	S

WORD PUZZLE 147

A quotation has been written in this diagram. Find the start letter and move from square to touching square until you have found it. What is the quotation and to whom is it attributed?

ANSWER 145

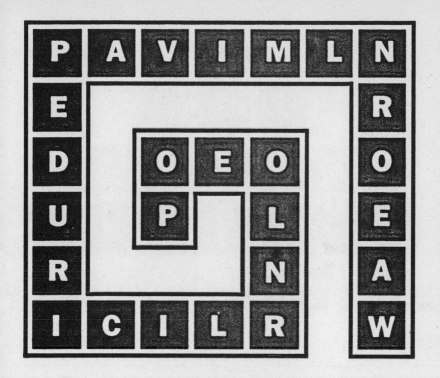

WORD PUZZLE 148

The names of three animals are to be found in the
diagram. The letters of the names are in the order
they normally appear. What are the animals?

ANSWER 166

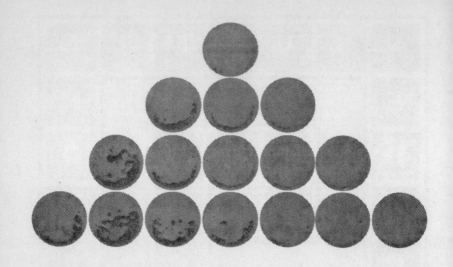

AAAEEIMMNNNORRST

WORD PUZZLE 149

Place the letters shown into the diagram in such a way that three words can be read across and one down the middle. What are the words?

ANSWER 114

WORD PUZZLE 150

Start at the bottom letter F and move from circle to
touching circle to the S at the top right. How many
different ways are there of collecting the nine
letters of FESTIVALS ?

ANSWER 125

1. **PHNTM F TH PR**

2. **CRSL**

3. **VT**

4. **STRLGHT XPRSS**

5. **TH SND F MSC**

6. **LS MSRBLS**

7. **CHSS**

8. **MSS SGN**

9. **RCKY HRRR SHW**

10. **CTS**

WORD PUZZLE 151

How well do you know stage musicals, old and new? Below you'll find some of them with their vowels missing. Can you work out what the musicals should be?

ANSWER 259

WORD PUZZLE 152

This fairy tale character was a bit of a bird brain.
Maybe that's how she got so confused.

ANSWER 271

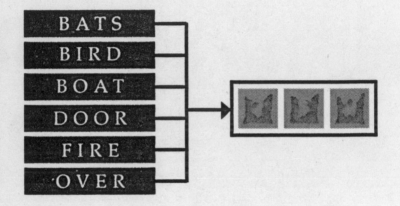

BATS
BIRD
BOAT
DOOR
FIRE
OVER

WORD PUZZLE 153

Which English word of three letters can be attached
to the back of the words shown in the diagram to
create six other words?

ANSWER 155

WORD PUZZLE 154

Select one letter from each of the segments.
When the correct letters have been found a word of
eight letters can be read clockwise.
What is the word?

ANSWER 196

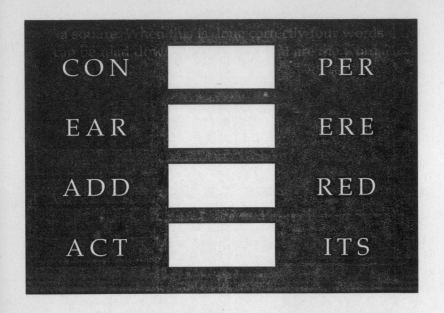

CON ☐ PER

EAR ☐ ERE

ADD ☐ RED

ACT ☐ ITS

WORD PUZZLE 155

Place two letters in the empty space which, when
added to the end of the words to the left and to the
beginning of the right, form other English words.
When this is completed another word
can be read down. What is the word?

ANSWER 144

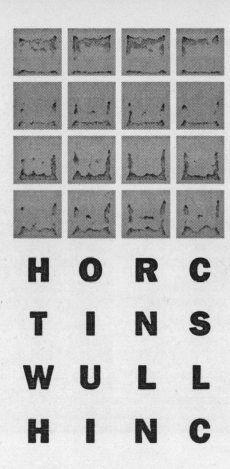

H	O	R	C
T	I	N	S
W	U	L	L
H	I	N	C

WORD PUZZLE 156

Take the letters and arrange them correctly in the column under which they appear. Once this has been done the name of a famous person will emerge. What is the name ?

ANSWER 186

STAR	?	WINE
CELL	?	MISSION
FAR	?	ASK
AMNESIA	?	REST
ANGLE	?	AFTER
MEN	?	NIT
CHILL	?	SLAM
TUB	?	HOE
SHIN	?	BONY

WORD PUZZLE 157

If you add the same letter to the end of the left word and the start of the right one on each line, you will find the name of a famous film star reading down. Who is he?

ANSWER 220

R	T	A	N	A
S	E	T	R	W
A	C	K	O	O
G	U	**C**	R	M
O	H	L	A	H
M	F	A	N	C
P	F	I	R	Y

WORD PUZZLE 158

Below you'll find the names of five birds which all start from the central C. The letters which make up the words are connected vertically, horizontally and diagonally. Not every letter is used and some may be used more than once. What are the birds?

ANSWER 261

WORD PUZZLE 159

Start at the bottom letter M and move from circle to touching circle to the S at the top right. How many different ways are there of collecting the nine letters of MAGAZINES?

ANSWER 177

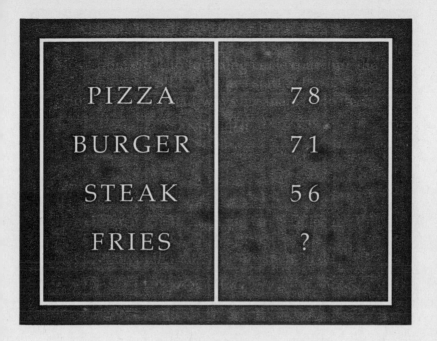

PIZZA	78
BURGER	71
STEAK	56
FRIES	?

WORD PUZZLE 160

On this list of stock the number of packets of each food are written . The numbers bear a relationship to the letters in the words. What should replace the question mark?

ANSWER 176

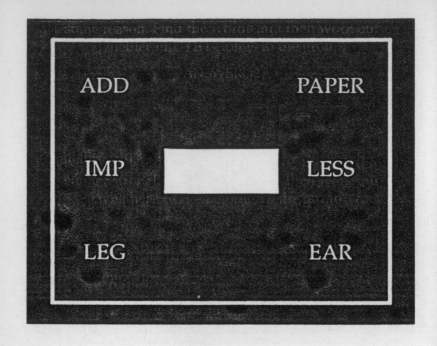

ADD		PAPER
IMP		LESS
LEG		EAR

WORD PUZZLE 161

Place an English word of THREE letters in the empty space. This word, when added to the end of the three words to the left and to the beginning of the three words to the right, will form six other words. What is the word?

ANSWER 124

WORD PUZZLE 162

Place one letter in the middle of this diagram. Four five-letter words can now be rearranged from each straight line of letters. What is the letter and what are the words?

ANSWER 165

CLFRN

DH

NBRSK

HW

LSK

WORD PUZZLE 163

The unpronounceable jumbles below are really
States in America without their vowels.
How many of them can you unravel?

ANSWER 276

DRAPERY	SPEND
COWARD	SAUCER
SPIGOT	CATAPULT
DOGGED	BICYCLE

WORD PUZZLE 164

All the words in the left-hand box have something in common. Which of the words in the right-hand box should join them?

ANSWER 264

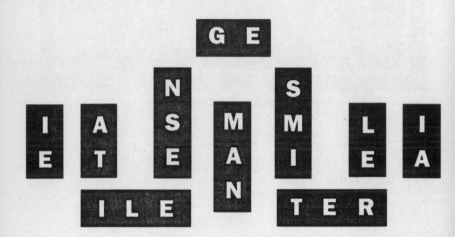

WORD PUZZLE 165

Arrange the tiles in this diagram so that they form
a square. When this is done correctly five words
can be read downwards and across.
What are the words?

ANSWER 113

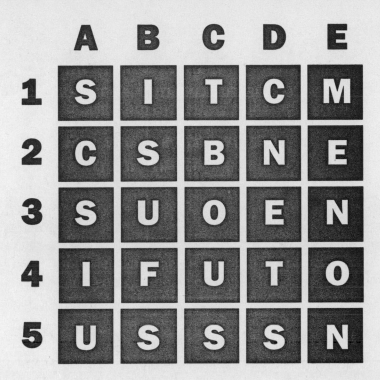

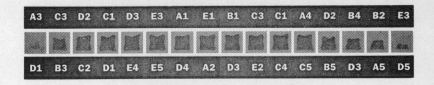

WORD PUZZLE 166

Select one of the two letters from the grid, in accordance with the reference shown, and place it in the word frame. When the correct letters have been chosen a sixteen-letter word can be read. What is the word?

ANSWER 206

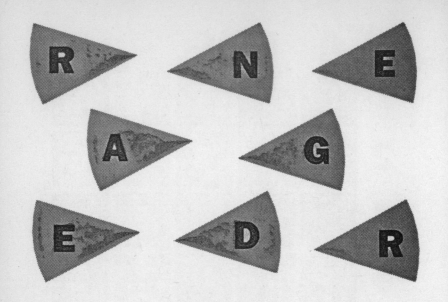

WORD PUZZLE 167

Make a circle out of these shapes.
When the correct circle has been found an English
word can be read clockwise. What is the word?

ANSWER 154

WORD PUZZLE 168

Move from circle to touching circle collecting the
letters of WAVE. Always start at the W.
How many different ways are there to do this?

ANSWER 195

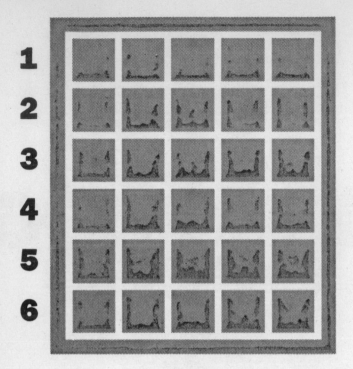

1. To move around quietly

2. Someone who says you were with them when the crime was committed.

3. You have these on fingers and toes.

4. Man who makes you laugh as his job.

5. Bird of prey.

6. A train runs on these.

WORD PUZZLE 169

All the answers to the clues below are five-letter words. When you have written them in the grid, you will be able to read the names of two signs of the zodiac down the first and last columns. Which ones?

ANSWER 216

WORD PUZZLE 170

Can you find a nine-letter word scrambled in the square? Clue: A bit jumpy.

ANSWER 248

BACON	BABES
GAMES	GIPSY
SUSHI	RESIN
PAPER	TALES
TRAIN	CAKES

WORD PUZZLE 171

Five of the words in the diagram are associated for some reason. Find the words and then work out whether CAFES belongs to the group.

ANSWER 143

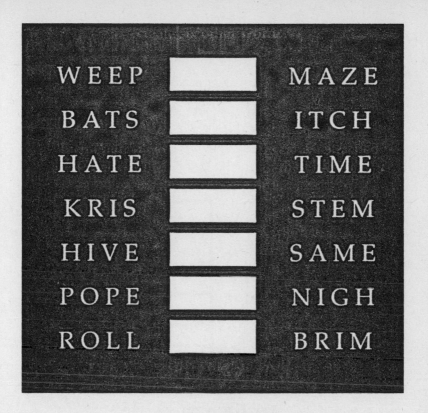

WEEP   MAZE

BATS   ITCH

HATE   TIME

KRIS   STEM

HIVE   SAME

POPE   NIGH

ROLL   BRIM

WORD PUZZLE 172

Change the first letter of each word to the left and
the right. Two other English words must be
formed. Place the letter used in the empty section.
When this has been completed for all the words
another English word can be read down.
What is the word?

ANSWER 185

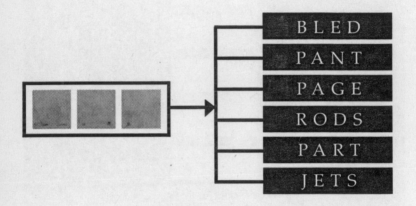

WORD PUZZLE 173

Which English word of three letters can be attached
to the front of the words shown in the diagram to
create six other words?

ANSWER 133

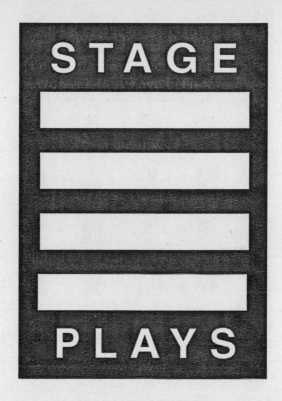

WORD PUZZLE 174

Complete the word ladder by changing one letter of each word per step. The newly created word must be found in the dictionary. What are the words to turn STAGE to PLAYS?

ANSWER 175

WORD PUZZLE 176

Take a letter from each country in turn
to make another 7 letter country.
Clue: It could feel a little chilly here!

ANSWER 231

1000 o 500 1 100 u 1000

100 a 500 1000 1 u 1000

a 100 a 500 e 1000 1 100

500 u 1000 1000 1 e 500

a 100 100 e 500 e 500

WORD PUZZLE 177

Look carefully at the following 'words'. If you replace the numbers with Roman numerals you should be able to read them easily.

ANSWER 265

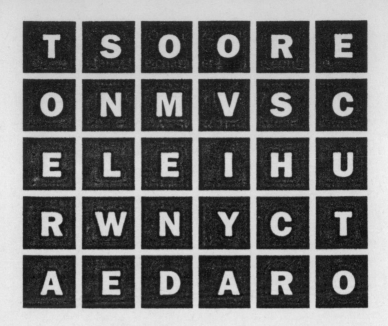

WORD PUZZLE 178

A quotation has been written in this diagram.
Find the start letter and move from square to
touching square until you have found it. What is
the quotation and to whom is it attributed?

ANSWER 123

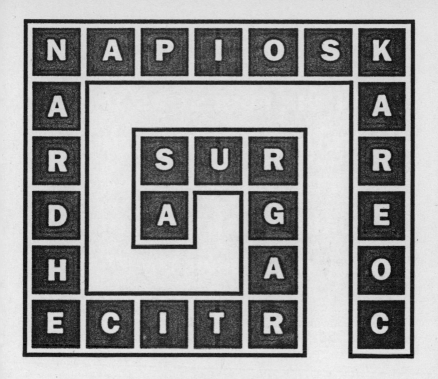

WORD PUZZLE 179

The names of three plants are to be found in the diagram. The letters of the names are in the order they normally appear. What are the plants?

ANSWER 164

IN THE FOREST AS THE
FRUIT • • • • • • THE
FURTIVE • • • • • •
LURKS IN ANTICIPATION
OF HIS VICTIM.

WORD PUZZLE 180

Two words using the same letters in their construction can be used to replace the dots in this sentence. The sentence will then make sense. Each dot is one letter. What are the words?

ANSWER 112

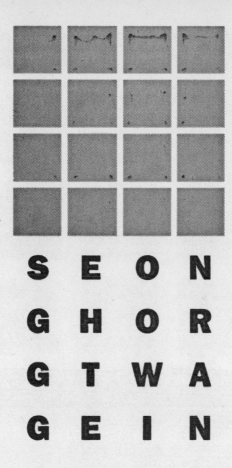

S E O N
G H O R
G T W A
G E I N

WORD PUZZLE 181

Take the letters and arrange them correctly in the column under which they appear. Once this has been done the name of a famous person will emerge. What is the name?

ANSWER 184

WORD PUZZLE 182

How may words of three letters or more can you find in this square? The computer found 102, but as you don't have a microchip in your head we don't expect you to get quite so many! A score of fifteen is good, twenty-five very good and forty or more excellent. What is the nine letter word?

ANSWER 236

HALLO		ASH
SCAMP		DEAL
AWAKE		EON
CAME		WE
ARISE		OR
ARE		KIN
PEA		EACH
BUS		OWL
JOSTLE		ARK
HOP		VENT
STRANGE		ANKLE

WORD PUZZLE 183

Reading down, the name of a well-known young actress should be revealed in the middle column which is currently empty. To discover her identity, it is useful for you to know that each letter of her name will help you create two brand new words on every line, the left one ending with the letter, the right one starting. Who is she?

ANSWER 272

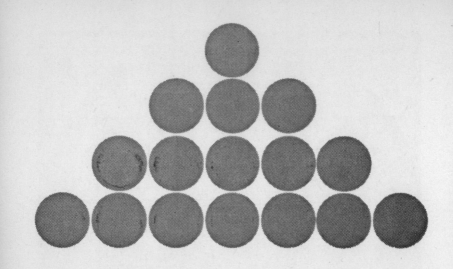

A A A B C D D E H I K L M N R Y

WORD PUZZLE 184

Place the letters shown into the diagram in such a way that three words can be read across and one down the middle. What are the words?

ANSWER 132

WORD PUZZLE 185

Select one letter from each of the segments.
When the correct letters have been found a word of
eight letters can be read clockwise.
What is the word?

ANSWER 194

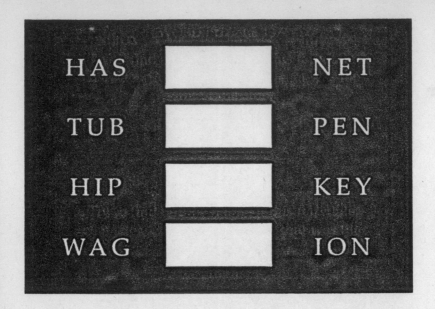

WORD PUZZLE 186

Place two letters in the empty space which, when
added to the end of the words to the left and to the
beginning of the right, form other English words.
When this is completed another word can be read
down. What is the word?

ANSWER 142

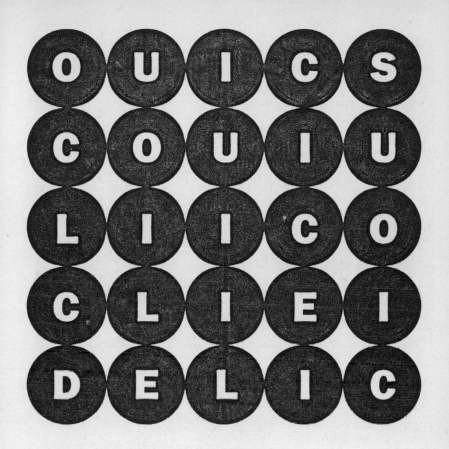

WORD PUZZLE 187

Start at the bottom letter D and move from circle to
touching circle to the S at the top right. How many
different ways are there of collecting the nine
letters of DELICIOUS?

ANSWER 205

VINCENT	CHAGALL
LEONARDO	PICASSO
PABLO	CONSTABLE
JOHN	DA VINCI
MARC	VAN GOGH

WORD PUZZLE 188

Danny Diablo has gone on a school outing to
the art gallery. His teacher prayed that, for once,
he would be good but within minutes of entering
the building he has switched round the names
of several famous artists. Can you rearrange
them before the warder notices and throws
the whole class out?

ANSWER 215

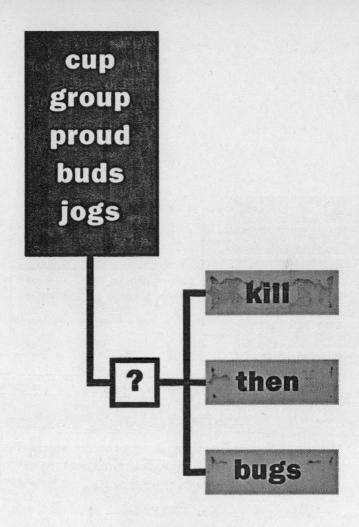

WORD PUZZLE 189

The words in the box have something in common.
Which of the following words should join them?

ANSWER 240

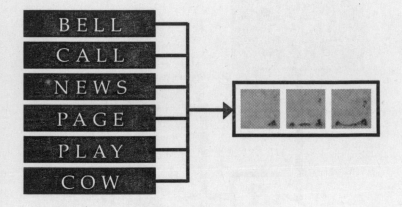

BELL
CALL
NEWS
PAGE
PLAY
COW

WORD PUZZLE 190

Which English word of three letters can be attached to the back of the words shown in the diagram to create six other words?

ANSWER 153

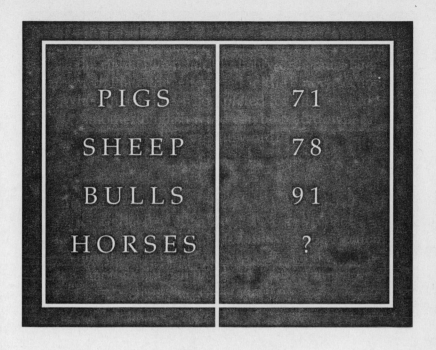

PIGS	71
SHEEP	78
BULLS	91
HORSES	?

WORD PUZZLE 191

On this list of farm stock the number of animals is written. The numbers bear a relationship to the letters in the words. What should replace the question mark?

ANSWER 174

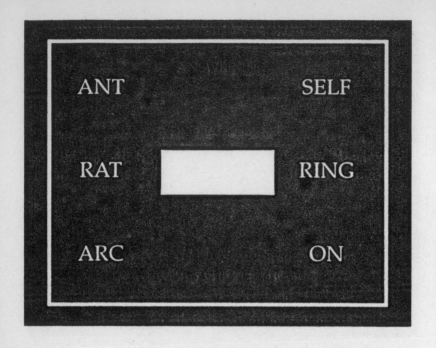

ANT	SELF
RAT	RING
ARC	ON

WORD PUZZLE 192

Place an English word of THREE letters in the empty space. This word, when added to the end of the three words to the left and to the beginning of the three words to the right, will form six other words. What is the word?

ANSWER 122

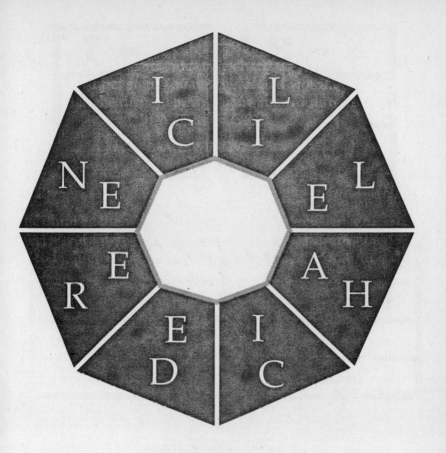

WORD PUZZLE 193

Place one letter in the middle of this diagram. Four
five-letter words can now be rearranged from each
straight line of letters. What is the letter and what
are the words?

ANSWER 163

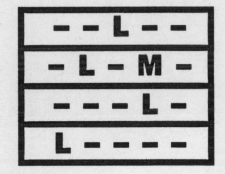

WORD PUZZLE 194

Can you fill in these blanks? In each puzzle the
letters missing are the same for every line.

ANSWER 268

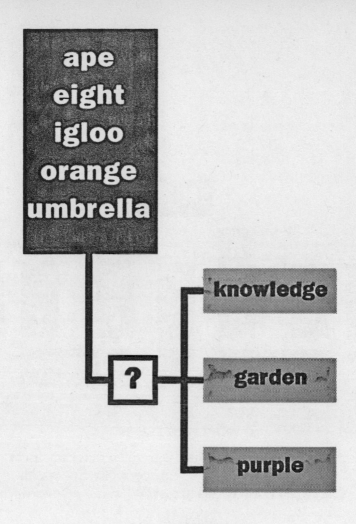

ape
eight
igloo
orange
umbrella

knowledge

garden

purple

?

WORD PUZZLE 195

The words in the box have been chosen
according to a simple system. Can any of the
words outside join them.

ANSWER 217

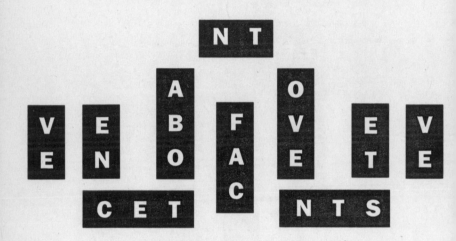

WORD PUZZLE 196

Arrange the tiles in this diagram so that they form
a square. When this is done correctly five words
can be read down and across. What are the words?

ANSWER 111

WORD PUZZLE 197

Select one of the two letters from the grid, in accordance with the reference shown, and place it in the word frame. When the correct letters have been chosen a sixteen-letter word can be read. What is the word?

ANSWER 204

WORD PUZZLE 198

Make a circle out of these shapes.
When the correct circle has been found an English
word can be read clockwise. What is the word?

ANSWER 152

WORD PUZZLE 199

Move from circle to touching circle collecting the
letters of BOAT. Always start at the B.
How many different ways are there to do this?

ANSWER 193

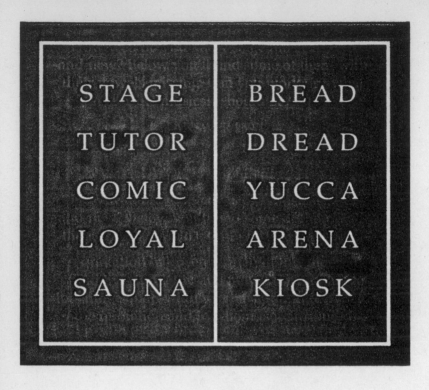

STAGE	BREAD
TUTOR	DREAD
COMIC	YUCCA
LOYAL	ARENA
SAUNA	KIOSK

WORD PUZZLE 200

Five of the words in the diagram are associated for some reason. Find the words and then work out whether WIDOW belongs to the group.

ANSWER 141

THIN		RAGE
SKIN		FIRS
WIFE		BUMP
SOUR		TANK
DARK		MOST
CHIP		WEAR
WILY		BATH

WORD PUZZLE 201

Change the first letter of each word to the left and the right. Two other English words must be formed. Place the letter used in the empty section. When this has been completed for all the words another English word can be read down. What is the word?

ANSWER 183

PALBEAM

HORNACE   **CAPLE**   **MASTLE**

BUNWOOD   **GALOWRED**

MONAR

COTTORY   **HICKAGE**

CEDASTERY

WORD PUZZLE 202

Here we have mixed the names of trees with the
names of places where people live. See if you can
untangle the resulting strange words.

ANSWER 239

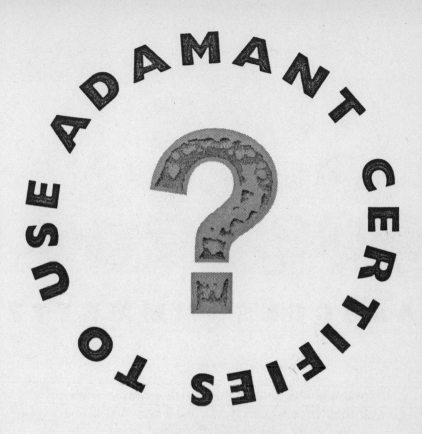

ADAMANT CERTIFIES TO USE

WORD PUZZLE 203

The words around the circle can be rearranged to
form the name of a country.
Clue: 51

ANSWER 267

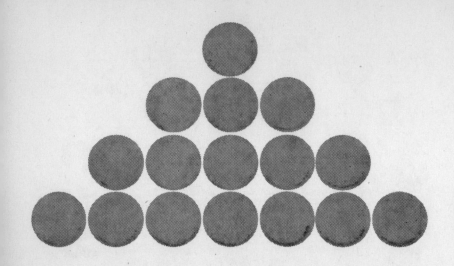

AAABCEEEHMMMRTTZ

WORD PUZZLE 204

Place the letters shown into the diagram in such a
way that three words can be read across and one
down the middle. What are the words?

ANSWER 131

WORD PUZZLE 205

Complete the word ladder by changing one letter of each word per step. The newly created word must be found in the dictionary. What are the words to turn DROP to FALL?

ANSWER 173

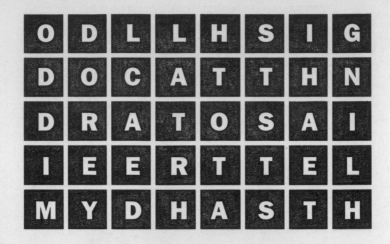

WORD PUZZLE 206

A quotation has been written in this diagram.
Find the start letter and move from square to
touching square until you have found it. What is
the quotation and to whom is it attributed?

ANSWER 121

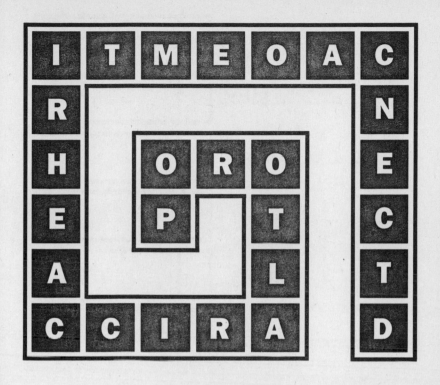

WORD PUZZLE 207

The names of three professions are to be found in
the diagram. The letters of the names are in the
order they normally appear.
What are the professions?

ANSWER 162

_ _ _ jump

_ _ _ _ site

_ _ _ _ storm

_ _ _ _ _ wave

_ _ _ _ _ days

_ _ _ _ _badge

WORD PUZZLE 208

Complete the phrases below, then write the missing
words in the grid with the first letter in the box.
You should be able to read a six-letter word down.
Clue: Fish

ANSWER 218

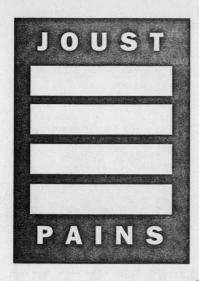

JOUST

PAINS

CLOCK

BREAD

WORD PUZZLE 209

Change the top word into the bottom one by
altering a letter each time and forming a
new word with each move.

ANSWER 222

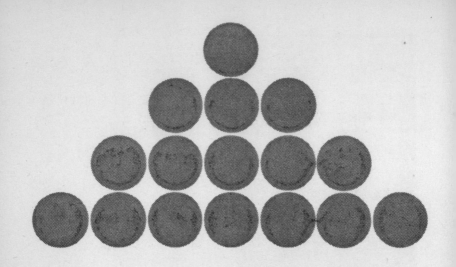

A B C C H I I N O O S T T T U

WORD PUZZLE 210

Place the letters shown into the diagram in such a
way that three words can be read across and one
down the middle. What are the words?

ANSWER 110

THE VALUABLE
SCIENTIFIC EQUIPMENT
WAS CAREFULLY • • • • • •
AND CHECKED BEFORE
BEING • • • • • • TO
THE OTHER SIDE OF
THE BUILDING.

WORD PUZZLE 211

Two words using the same letters in their
construction can be used to replace the dots in this
sentence. The sentence will then make sense. Each
dot is one letter. What are the words?

ANSWER 203

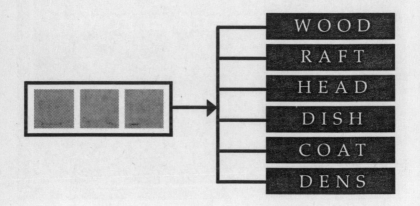

WORD PUZZLE 212

Which English word of three letters can be attached
to the front of the words shown in the diagram to
create six other words?

ANSWER 151

WORD PUZZLE 213

Select one letter from each of the segments.
When the correct letters have been found a word of
eight letters can be read clockwise.
What is the word?

ANSWER 192

DI	VER	FLAB
SION	DI	IN
TIC	SUS	BU
MAN	PER	MEN
AB	RO	REAU
NEWS	TUDE	BER
TEER	CATE	CRAT
NANCE	VOL	DO
LON	GAST	UN
PA	GI	TE

WORD PUZZLE 214

Below you will see thirty syllables. If you rearrange them you'll find that, using each syllable only once, they will make up ten three-syllable words.
What are the words?

ANSWER 245

N	O	L
I	S	S
E	S	E

WORD PUZZLE 215

Use all the letters in the grid twice to give you two nine-letter words.
The clue is: SILENT LADY KILLERS

ANSWER 247

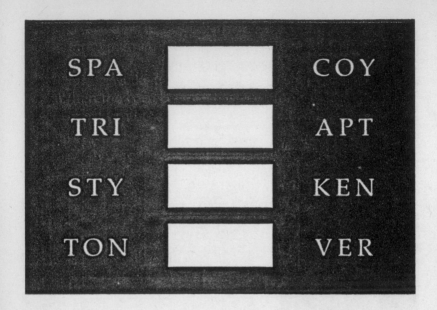

SPA		COY
TRI		APT
STY		KEN
TON		VER

WORD PUZZLE 216

Place two letters in the empty space which, when
added to the end of the words to the left and to the
beginning of the right, form other English words.
When this is completed another word
can be read down. What is the word?

ANSWER 140

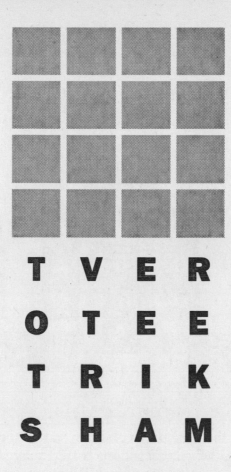

T V E R

O T E E

T R I K

S H A M

WORD PUZZLE 217

Take the letters and arrange them correctly in the
column under which they appear. Once this has
been done the name of a film will emerge.
What is it?

ANSWER 182

WORD PUZZLE 218

Arrange the tiles in this diagram so that they form a square. When this is done correctly five words can be read down and across. What are the words?

ANSWER 130

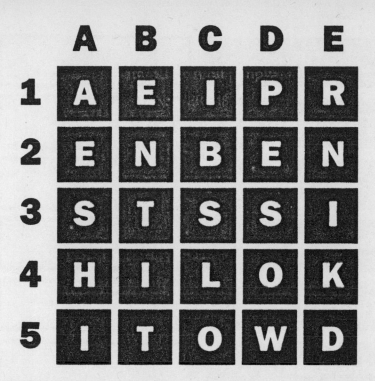

	A	**B**	**C**	**D**	**E**
1	A	E	I	P	R
2	E	N	B	E	N
3	S	T	S	S	I
4	H	I	L	O	K
5	I	T	O	W	D

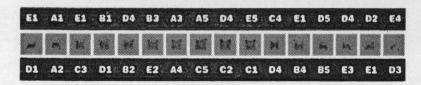

| E1 | A1 | E1 | B1 | D4 | B3 | A3 | A5 | D4 | E5 | C4 | E1 | D5 | D4 | D2 | E4 |
| D1 | A2 | C3 | D1 | B2 | E2 | A4 | C5 | C2 | C1 | D4 | B4 | B5 | E3 | E1 | D3 |

WORD PUZZLE 219

Select one of the two letters from the grid, in
accordance with the reference shown, and place it
in the word frame. When the correct letters have
been chosen a sixteen-letter word can be read.
What is the word?

ANSWER 172

Natation	
Toxophily	
Soccer	
Track & Field	
Equestrianism	
Blade Balance	

WORD PUZZLE 220

The following clues will give you the name of six sports. Read the first letters of the words in order and you will be transported to Africa.

ANSWER 232

cease

hares

sloth

beach

again

brown

abbey

frown

green

beans

acids

drama

WORD PUZZLE 221

Five of the words below are related in some way.
Discover which ones they are and see if
brass could join them.

ANSWER 221

THE LANGUAGE USED
BY THE • • • • • • AT
THE BASEBALL GAME
WAS SO • • • • • •
IT WAS SCARCELY
UNDERSTANDABLE.

WORD PUZZLE 222

Two words using the same letters in their
construction can be used to replace the dots in this
sentence. The sentence will then make sense. Each
dot is one letter. What are the words?

ANSWER 120

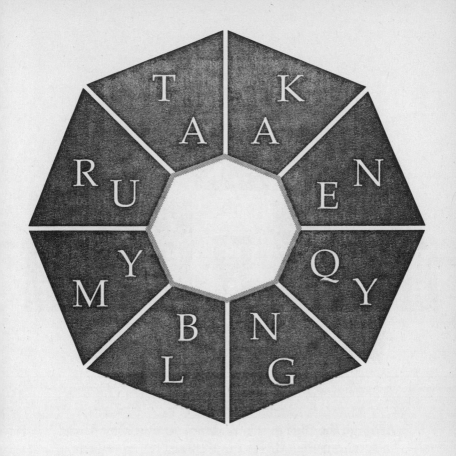

WORD PUZZLE 223

Place one letter in the middle of this diagram. Four five-letter words can now be rearranged from each straight line of letters. What is the letter and what are the words?

ANSWER 161

WORD PUZZLE 224

Arrange the tiles in this diagram so that they form
a square. When this is done correctly five words
can be read downwards and across.
What are the words?

ANSWER 109

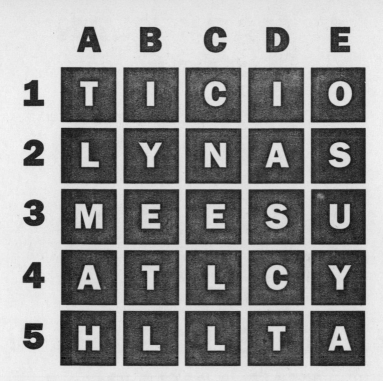

	A	**B**	**C**	**D**	**E**
1	T	I	C	I	O
2	L	Y	N	A	S
3	M	E	E	S	U
4	A	T	L	C	Y
5	H	L	L	T	A

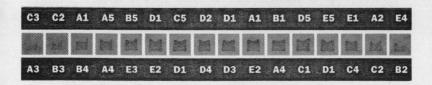

C3	C2	A1	A5	B5	D1	C5	D2	D1	A1	B1	D5	E5	E1	A2	E4

A3	B3	B4	A4	E3	E2	D1	D4	D3	E2	A4	C1	D1	C4	C2	B2

WORD PUZZLE 225

Select one of the two letters from the grid, in accordance with the reference shown, and place it in the word frame. When the correct letters have been chosen a sixteen-letter word can be read. What is the word?

ANSWER 202

1. MASK PLAN FIRED

2. SITED HARM

3. MAULED TO REJOIN

4. BOSS DEFILER V THE LUSTRE

WORD PUZZLE 226

Turn the anagrams below into four classic works
of English literature. Name the authors too.
Clue: there is a hint to the theme of the books
in the anagram.

ANSWER 237

HOAX

THAW

ATOM

AVOW

IOTA

TAXI

MIAOW

WORD PUZZLE 227

Look at the following list of words.
There is something special about them.
Can you work out what it is?

ANSWER 224

WORD PUZZLE 228

Make a circle out of these shapes.
When the correct circle has been found an English
word can be read clockwise. What is the word?

ANSWER 150

WORD PUZZLE 229

Move from circle to touching circle collecting the
letters of FACE. Always start at the F.
How many different ways are there to do this?

ANSWER 191

HYMNS	LIGHT
SHRUB	FILMS
PIZZA	QUEEN
ANKLE	FLAME
PASTA	INDEX

WORD PUZZLE 230

Six of the words in the diagram are associated for
some reason. Find the words and then work out
whether GLOBE belongs to the group.

ANSWER 139

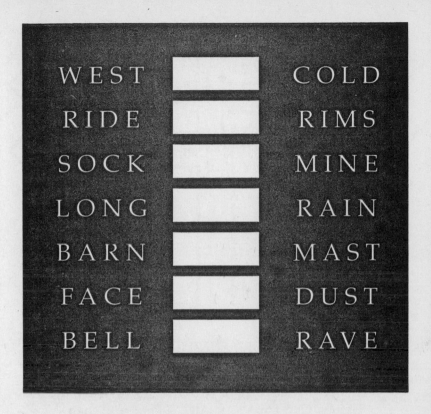

WEST		COLD
RIDE		RIMS
SOCK		MINE
LONG		RAIN
BARN		MAST
FACE		DUST
BELL		RAVE

WORD PUZZLE 231

Change the first letter of each word to the left and
the right. Two other English words must be
formed. Place the letter used in the empty section.
When this has been completed for all the words
another English word can be read down.
What is the word?

ANSWER 181

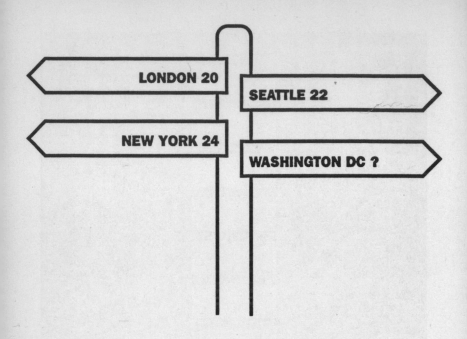

WORD PUZZLE 232

Look at the signpost below. The distances given are related, by some form of twisted logic, to the place names. Can you work out the logic and then replace the question mark with the correct distance? If you want a clue, remember the words have consonants and vowels.

ANSWER 234

A	X	M	I	R	R	O	R	H
B	E	L	D	D	A	S	B	A
W	I	L	R	T	V	E	S	N
P	O	C	E	T	L	S	E	D
E	E	U	Y	L	J	B	K	L
M	E	D	S	C	A	L	O	E
A	G	W	A	N	L	M	P	B
R	E	V	Q	L	R	E	S	A
F	N	I	A	H	C	T	Y	R
D	R	A	U	G	D	U	M	S

1. Reflector
2. Steering device
3. Wheel parts
4. Foot rest
5. Driver
6. Splash preventor
7. Seat
8. Ringer
9. Bike
10. Skeleton

WORD PUZZLE 233

The clues will help you to find ten hidden words all to do with cycling. The words may be written in any direction and the grid contains dummy letters.

ANSWER 244

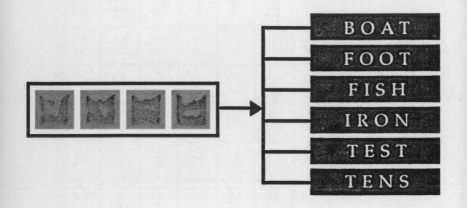

WORD PUZZLE 234

Which English word of four letters can be attached
to the front of the words shown in the diagram to
create six other words?

ANSWER 129

WORD PUZZLE 235

Complete the word ladder by changing one letter
of each word per step. The newly created word
must be found in the dictionary. What are the
words to turn PORT to SHIP?

ANSWER 171

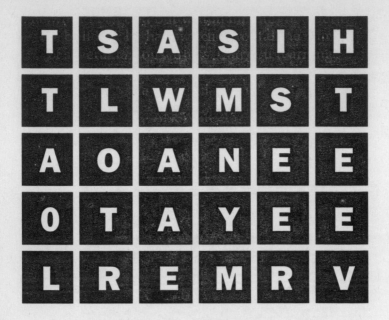

WORD PUZZLE 236

A quotation has been written in this diagram.
Find the start letter and move from square to
touching square until you have found it. What is
the quotation and to whom is it attributed?

ANSWER 119

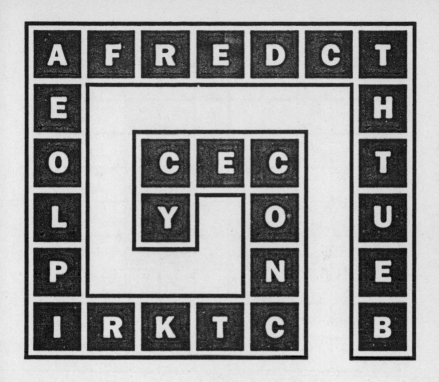

WORD PUZZLE 237

The names of three insects are to be found in the
diagram. The letters of the names are in the order
they normally appear. What are the insects?

ANSWER 160

ACROSS

1. Tall pole on a ship which supports the sail (4)
6. A person who has no parents (6)
8. Father (2)
9. Part of something (4)
10. It helps you to draw straight lines (5)
12. Tea, lemonade and orange juice are these (6)
13. To carry out something (2)
14. This would be steep to walk up (6)
16. A male deer (4)
18. You use this on your hair to make it stay in place (3)
19. A baby horse (4)
21. You open and close this (4)
23. A narrow passageway (8)

DOWN

1. The early part of the day (7)
2. I am, you _ _ _ (3)
3. A flash (5)
4. A type of bird (6)
5. An outlaw (6)
7. You use this to mend your clothes (6)
11. You fasten this in your hair to make it curl (6)
15. An eskimo's home (5)
16. Water in a plant (3)
17. As well (4)
19. A long way (3)
20. To unite by addition (3)
22. Either, _ _ (2)

WORD PUZZLE 238

ANSWER 223

anteater
encyclopedia
ahead
astrology
red
confederation
hopeless
acrimony
eagles
nausea
acids
telephone
sight
azalea

WORD PUZZLE 239

Five of the words below are related. Discover
which ones they are and then see if confidence
could join them.

ANSWER 257

A A A B C C E H N N O O R S S T

WORD PUZZLE 240

Place the letters shown into the diagram in such a way that three words can be read across and one down the middle. What are the words?

ANSWER 108

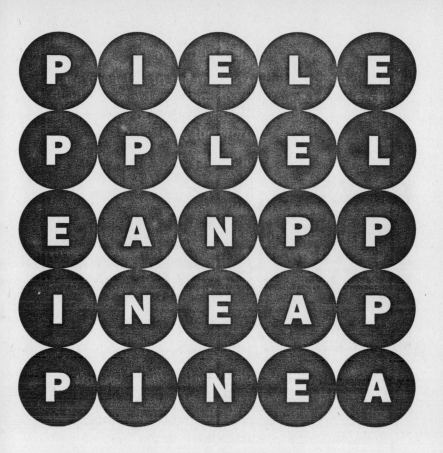

WORD PUZZLE 241

Start at the bottom letter P and move from circle to touching circle to the E at the top right. How many different ways are there of collecting the nine letters of PINEAPPLE?

ANSWER 201

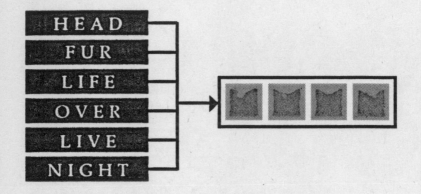

WORD PUZZLE 242

Which English word of four letters can be attached
to the back of the words shown in the diagram to
create six other words?

ANSWER 149

WORD PUZZLE 243

Select one letter from each of the segments.
When the correct letters have been found a word of
eight letters can be read clockwise.
What is the word?

ANSWER 190

		8			22	16	10	6	4	7	4	3
25	8	11	11	6		8		16		21	7	
7		7		16		10			14		21	11
26	7	4	21		1		22	24	15	11		23
7			7		4	11			7			9
4			18	16	16		9	6	22	5		6
9	20	24	11		26				13	9	6	
	11			10	9	2	5	6		12		16
	8		2	7	6	11			17	11	7	20
			21		10	7	9	24				20
7	4	6		11		6			15		9	
	7		16			24		12	11	25	6	
	19	15	10	2	24	11				16		

1	2	3	4 R	5	6 T	7	8 W	9	10 N	11 E	12	13
14	15	16 O	17	18	19	20	21	22	23	24 L	25	26

WORD PUZZLE 244

Your task here is to work out which letter of the
alphabet is represented by each of the numbers 1 to
26. To help you, we've given you a few letters to
start you off. When you work out what the numbers represent, write them in the reference grid at
the bottom. The completed puzzle will look like a
filled-in crossword, featuring only genuine words.

ANSWER 241

A
B B
R R R
A A A A
C C C C C
A A A A A A
D D D D D D D
A A A A A A A A
B B B B B B B B B
R R R R R R R R R R
A A A A A A A A A A A

WORD PUZZLE 245

In the diagram you see the magic word Abracadabra spelt out as a pyramid. There are various paths from top to bottom but how many ways can you discover to spell the trick word?

ANSWER 255

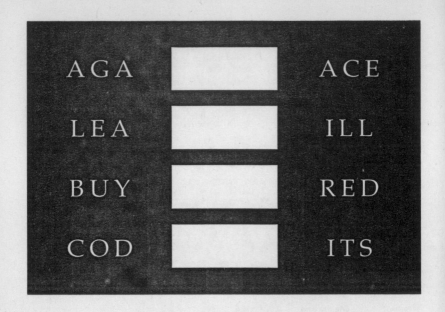

WORD PUZZLE 246

Place two letters in the empty space which, when added to the words to the left and to the right, form other English words. When this is completed another word can be read down.
What is the word?

ANSWER 138

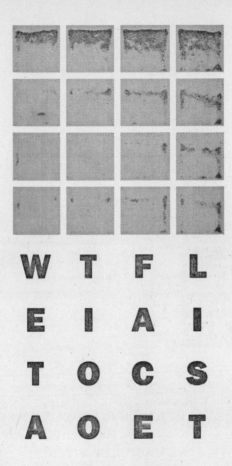

W	T	F	L
E	I	A	I
T	O	C	S
A	O	E	T

WORD PUZZLE 247

Take the letters and arrange them correctly in the column under which they appear. Once this has been done the name of a novel and a movie will emerge. What is it?

ANSWER 180

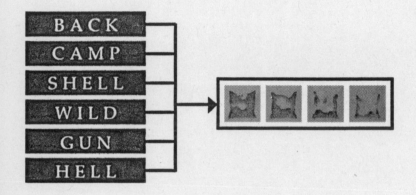

WORD PUZZLE 248

Which English word of four letters can be attached
to the back of the words shown in the diagram to
create six other words?

ANSWER 128

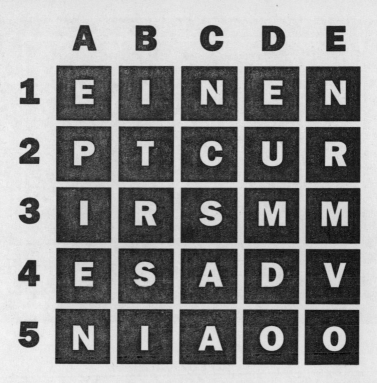

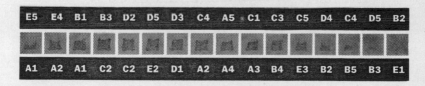

WORD PUZZLE 249

Select one of the two letters from the grid, in accordance with the reference shown, and place it in the word frame. When the correct letters have been chosen a sixteen-letter word can be read. What is the word?

ANSWER 170

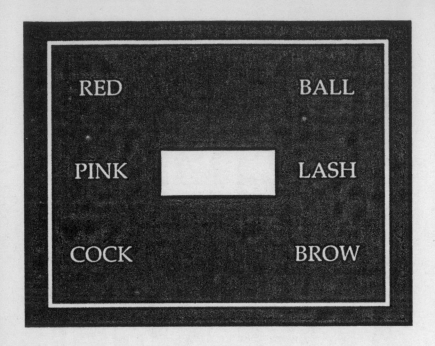

RED   BALL

PINK   LASH

COCK   BROW

WORD PUZZLE 250

Place an English word of THREE letters in the
empty space. This word, when added to the end of
the three words to the left and to the beginning of
the three words to the right, will form six other
words. What is the word?

ANSWER 118

WORD PUZZLE 251

Place one letter in the middle of this diagram.
Four five-letter words can now be rearranged from
each straight line of letters. What is the letter and what
are the words?

ANSWER 159

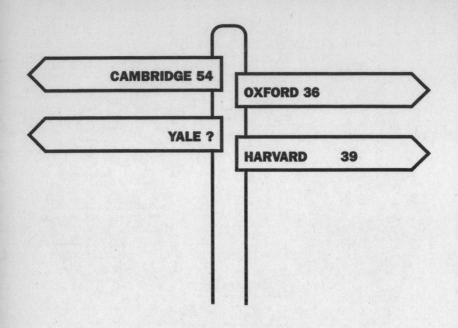

WORD PUZZLE 252

Look at the signpost below. The distances given are
related, by some form of twisted logic, to the place
names. Can you work out the logic and then
replace the question mark with the correct distance?

ANSWER 277

fireball

ready

it

yellow

transubstantiation

hamburger

analysis

anything

bottomless

acolyte

rival

rivet

golf

WORD PUZZLE 253

Five of the words below are related. Discover which
ones they are and then see if heady could join them.

ANSWER 246

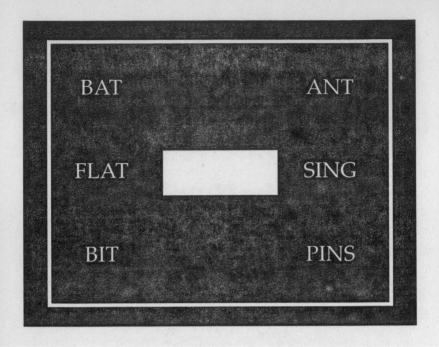

WORD PUZZLE 254

Place an English word of THREE letters in the empty space. This word, when added to the end of the three words to the left and to the beginning of the three words to the right, will form six other words. What is the word?

ANSWER 107

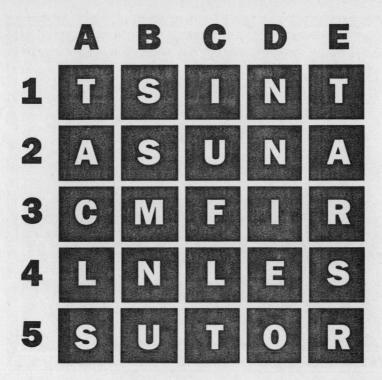

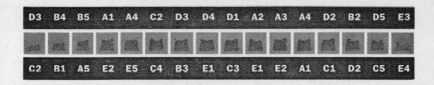

WORD PUZZLE 255

Select one of the two letters from the grid, in accordance with the reference shown, and place it in the word frame. When the correct letters have been chosen a sixteen-letter word can be read. What is the word?

ANSWER 200

THE CAVE MAN SAT

IN FRONT OF THE FIRE,

HOLDING A PIECE OF

• • • • • ON HIS KNEE,

ON WHICH WAS TO

BE FOUND SOME

• • • • • FOOD.

WORD PUZZLE 256

Two words using the same letters in their construction can be used to replace the dots in this sentence. The sentence will then make sense. Each dot is one letter. What are the words?

ANSWER 148

WORD PUZZLE 257

Move from circle to touching circle collecting the
letters of DIET. Always start at the D.
How many different ways are there to do this?

ANSWER 189

SIREN	SWORD
DENIM	VASES
WIDOW	FOCUS
TIARA	LOTUS
MELON	RUPEE

WORD PUZZLE 258

Five of the words in the diagram are associated for some reason. Find the words and then work out whether VISOR belongs to the group.

ANSWER 137

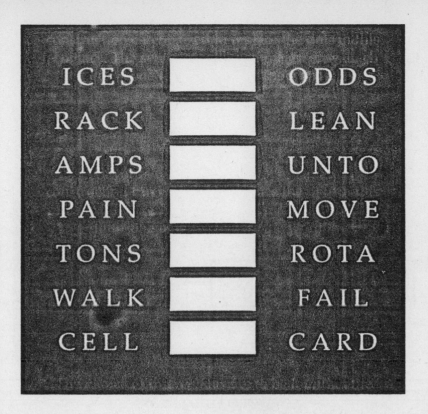

ICES		ODDS
RACK		LEAN
AMPS		UNTO
PAIN		MOVE
TONS		ROTA
WALK		FAIL
CELL		CARD

WORD PUZZLE 259

Change the first letter of each word to the left and
the right. Two other English words must be
formed. Place the letter used in the empty section.
When this has been completed for all the words
another English word can be read down.
What is the word?

ANSWER 179

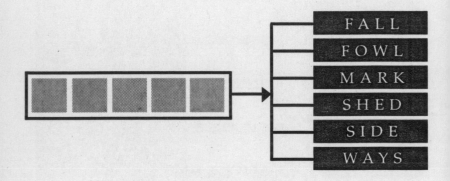

FALL
FOWL
MARK
SHED
SIDE
WAYS

WORD PUZZLE 260

Which English word of five letters can be attached
to the front of the words shown in the diagram to
create six other words?

ANSWER 127

WORD PUZZLE 261

Complete the word ladder by changing one letter of each word per step. The newly created word must be found in the dictionary. What are the words to turn GRAPE to PEACH?

ANSWER 169

D	N	O	T	S	K
E	F	W	H	E	A
R	R	O	H	E	M
G	R	E	S	C	E
T	A	B	A	E	N

WORD PUZZLE 262

A proverb has been written in this diagram. Find the start letter and move from square to touching square until you have found it. What is it?

ANSWER 117

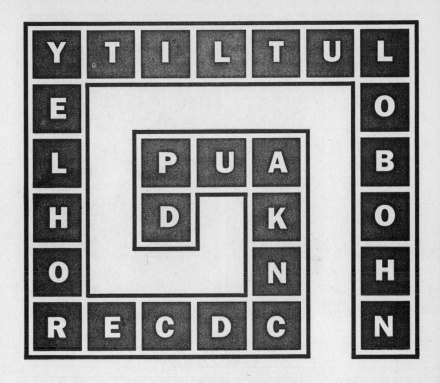

WORD PUZZLE 263
The names of three flowers are to be found in the diagram. The letters of the names are in the order they normally appear. What are the flowers?

ANSWER 158

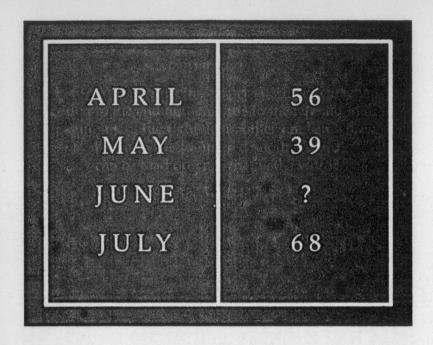

APRIL	56
MAY	39
JUNE	?
JULY	68

WORD PUZZLE 264

The diagram shows the sunshine hours in England for four months. The numbers bear a relationship to the letters in the words. What should replace the question mark?

ANSWER 106

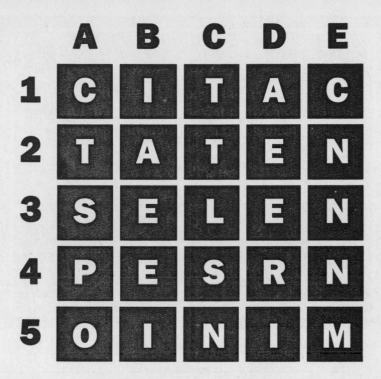

	A	B	C	D	E
1	C	I	T	A	C
2	T	A	T	E	N
3	S	E	L	E	N
4	P	E	S	R	N
5	O	I	N	I	M

| B5 | E2 | D1 | E2 | A3 | A1 | A5 | B4 | C2 | B1 | E1 | B3 | D2 | A2 | D5 | B5 |
| C1 | D4 | C1 | D3 | D4 | A4 | B2 | E4 | B4 | E3 | E3 | B5 | C5 | C4 | D1 | C3 |

WORD PUZZLE 265

Select one of the two letters from the grid, in accordance with the reference shown, and place it in the word frame. When the correct letters have been chosen a sixteen-letter word can be read. What is the word?

ANSWER 199

THE WEIGHT LIFTER,
ALTHOUGH VERY
• • • • • •, FAILED IN
HIS ATTEMPT BECAUSE
OF HIS • • • • • •
APPROACH.

WORD PUZZLE 266

Two words using the same letters in their construction can be used to replace the dots in this sentence. The sentence will then make sense. Each dot is one letter. What are the words?

ANSWER 147

	A	**B**	**C**	**D**	**E**
1	R	R	M	O	E
2	R	X	I	U	N
3	E	E	T	D	T
4	S	I	E	R	L
5	S	C	A	A	T

E1 D1 C3 D4 D5 E5 E2 A1 A4 A3 C2 E3 D2 C2 B4 E4

C1 B2 E2 E3 C4 D3 B3 E1 A2 A5 A4 C3 B1 D3 C5 B5

WORD PUZZLE 267

Select one of the two letters from the grid, in accordance with the reference shown, and place it in the word frame. When the correct letters have been chosen a sixteen-letter word can be read. What is the word?

ANSWER 188

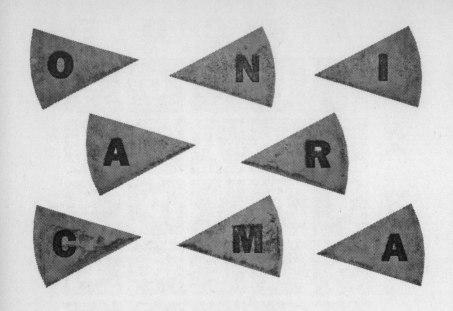

WORD PUZZLE 268

Make a circle out of these shapes. When the correct
circle has been found aword can be read
clockwise. What is the word?

ANSWER 136

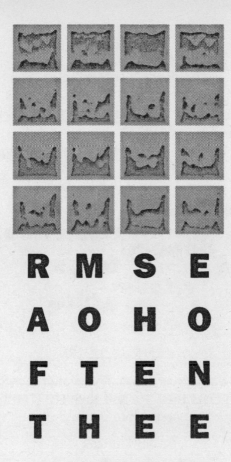

R M S E

A O H O

F T E N

T H E E

WORD PUZZLE 269

Take the letters and arrange them correctly in the column under which they appear. Once this has been done the name of a movie will emerge. What is it?

ANSWER 178

ziggurat average

ear gizmo

onomatopoeia introduction

uncle xylophone

classic

hangman numerical

depend force

grass white

WORD PUZZLE 270

Five of the words below are related. Discover
which ones they are and then see if ability
could join them.

ANSWER 269

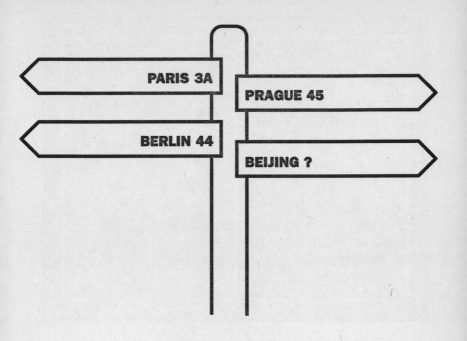

WORD PUZZLE 271

Look at the signpost below. The distances given are related, by some form of twisted logic, to the place names. Can you work out the logic and then replace the question mark with the correct distance?

ANSWER 251

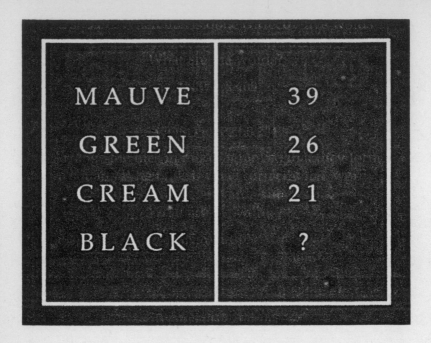

MAUVE	39
GREEN	26
CREAM	21
BLACK	?

WORD PUZZLE 272

On this list of four colours the numbers bear a
relationship to the letters in the words. What
should replace the question mark?

ANSWER 126

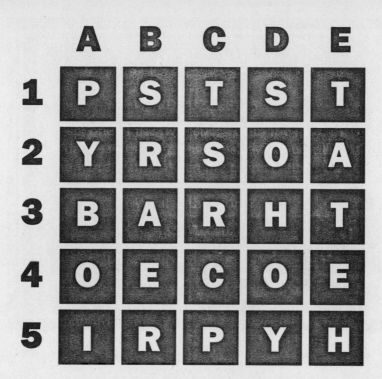

	A	B	C	D	E
1	P	S	T	S	T
2	Y	R	S	O	A
3	B	A	R	H	T
4	O	E	C	O	E
5	I	R	P	Y	H

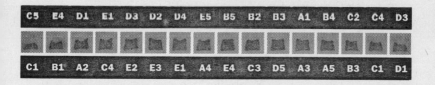

C5 E4 D1 E1 D3 D2 D4 E5 B5 B2 B3 A1 B4 C2 C4 D3

C1 B1 A2 C4 E2 E3 E1 A4 E4 C3 D5 A3 A5 B3 C1 D1

WORD PUZZLE 273

Select one of the two letters from the grid, in
accordance with the reference shown, and place it
in the word frame. When the correct letters have
been chosen a sixteen-letter word can be read.
What is the word?

ANSWER 168

THE PYTHON WOUND

• • • • • • AROUND

THE VICTIM AS IT

ATTEMPTED TO • • • • • •

IT TO DEATH.

WORD PUZZLE 274

Two words using the same letters in their construction can be used to replace the dots in this sentence. The sentence will then make sense. Each dot is one letter. What are the words?

ANSWER 116

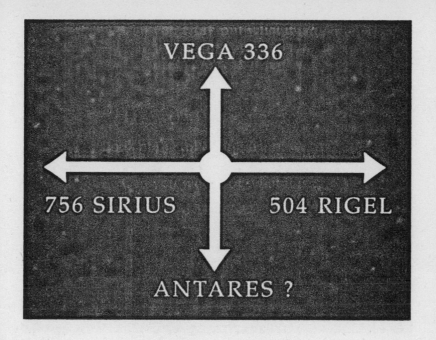

WORD PUZZLE 275

The diagram shows the light years to various stars.
The numbers bear a relationship to the letters in
the words. What should replace the question mark?

ANSWER 157

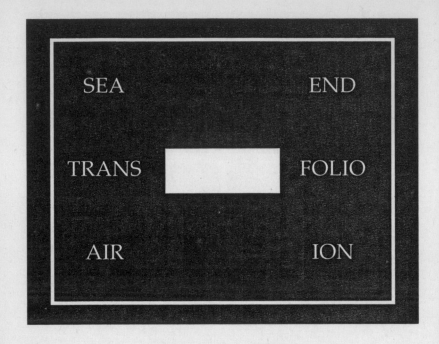

SEA   END

TRANS   [   ]   FOLIO

AIR   ION

WORD PUZZLE 276

Place an English word of FOUR letters in the
empty space. This word, when added to the end of
the three words to the left and to the beginning of
the three words to the right, will form six other
words. What is the word?

ANSWER 105

WORD PUZZLE 277

Select one letter from each of the segments.
When the correct letters have been found a word of
eight letters can be read clockwise.
What is the word?

ANSWER 198

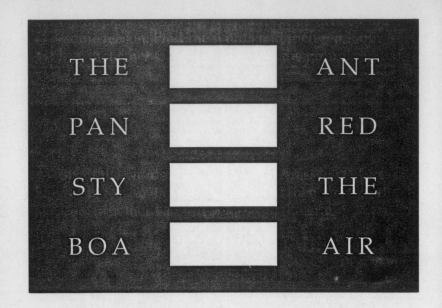

THE		ANT
PAN		RED
STY		THE
BOA		AIR

WORD PUZZLE 278

Place two letters in the empty space which, when
added to the words to the left and to the right,
form other English words. When this is completed
another word can be read down.
What is the word?

ANSWER 146

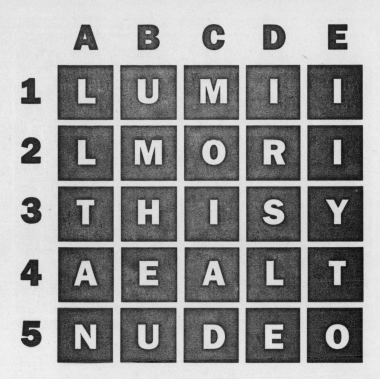

	A	B	C	D	E
1	L	U	M	I	I
2	L	M	O	R	I
3	T	H	I	S	Y
4	A	E	A	L	T
5	N	U	D	E	O

| C1 | B1 | A2 | B1 | E2 | B2 | C3 | A4 | E4 | E1 | C5 | A5 | C2 | D1 | D2 | E3 |

| E1 | A1 | D4 | A3 | C1 | D1 | A5 | A2 | A1 | D5 | E5 | B3 | C4 | B5 | D3 | B4 |

WORD PUZZLE 279

Select one of the two letters from the grid, in accordance with the reference shown, and place it in the word frame. When the correct letters have been chosen a sixteen-letter word can be read. What is the word?

ANSWER 187

IN THE FOREST FIRE

THE UNDERGROWTH

• • • • • • • • IN THE

FLAMES AS THE

TREE • • • • • • • .

WORD PUZZLE 280

Two words using the same letters in their construction can be used to replace the dots in this sentence. The sentence will then make sense. Each dot is one letter. What are the words?

ANSWER 135

The
BRAINTEASERS
Word
Puzzles
Book

ANSWERS

1. Ohm, Stoop, Respond, and Chop.

2. Word, Oboe, Rode, and Deep.

3. Mow, Jewel, Blanket, and Down.

4. Back, Aeon, Cove, and Knew.

5. Ivy, Geese, Embrace, and Over.

6. Yard, Afar, Race, and Drew.

7. Fir, First, Firearm, and Fire.

8. Stop, Tame, Omen, and Pent.

9. Lid, Valid, Quality, and Will.

10. Tide, Idea, Deer, and Ears

11. Fire.

12. Rulers have no authority from God to do mischief. Jonathan Mayhew.

13. Bird.

14. The first casualty when war comes is truth. Hiram Johnson.

15. Well.

16. All animals are equal but some animals are more equal than others. George Orwell.

17. Like.

18. If you can't stand the heat keep out of the kitchen. President Harry Truman.

19. Den.

20. When you have to kill a man it costs nothing to be polite. Winston Churchill.

21. Rugged and Grudge.

22. Low.

23. Misunderstanding.

24. Buck.

25. 192. Each vowel is worth 6 and each consonant 8. The vowels are added together, as are the consonants. The totals are then multiplied.

26. Foot.

27. Brides and Debris.

28. Hand.

29. 21 ways.

30. Moon.

31. Tolerate.

32. Flute does not belong to the group. The five associated words are Decoy, Steam, Tulip, Abbey, and Hippo. The first two letters of each word are in alphabetical order.

33. Delegate.

34. 12 ways.

35. Imposter.

36. 8 ways.

37. Operator.

38. 9 ways.

39. Reunites.

40. Shell does not belong to the group. The linked words are Beast, Decor, Heron, Human, Pilaf, and Round. The first and last letter position in the alphabet totals 22.

41. Daffodil.

42. Nest.

43. Baseball.

44. Cast.

45. Woodbine.

46. Band.

47. Taxpayer.

48. Step.

49. Aardvark.

50. House.

51. Kindness.

52. B. To give Elbow, Orbit, Habit, and Noble.

53. Satinwood, Jacaranda, and Greengage.

54. A. To give Koala, Peace, Shade, and Whale.

55. Cannelloni, Macaroni, and Spaghetti.

56. J. To give Enjoy, Major, Rajah, and Dojos.

57. Champagne, Chocolate, and Orangeade.

58. H. To give Abhor, Ethic, Ochre, and Usher.

59. Harmonium, Accordion, Piano, and Tuba.

60. P. To give Capon, Hippo, Imply, and Paper.

61. Argentina, Australia, and Indonesia.

62. G. To give Angel, Anger, Cigar, and Logic.

63. 27. Each vowel is worth 2 and each consonant 3. The totals of the vowels and consonants are added.

64. Loon, Loop, Poop, Pomp, Pump.

65. 20. Each vowel is worth 4 and each consonant 2. The totals of the vowels and consonants are added.

66. Pong, Pang, Rang, Rant, Cant.

67. Summer Vacations.

68. Raver, Raves, Paves, Pares, Bares, Barks.

69. 57. Each letter is given its positional value in the alphabet and these are added together.

70. Shop, Shoe, Sloe, Floe, Flee, Free.

71. 108. Each vowel in the name is worth 10 and each consonant is worth 22. These are all added together to give the distance.

72. Sleds, Slews, Slows, Glows, Grows, Gross.

73. Benjamin Franklin.

74. Gesture.

75. Dances with Wolves.

76. Rainbow.

77. The Spy Who Loved Me.

78. Emerald.

79. Oscar Hammerstein.

80. Magenta.

81. Mary, Queen of Scots.

82. Crimson.

83. Nineteen.

84. 17 ways.

85. Journals.

86. Style belongs to the group. The linked words are

Abyss, Buyer, Coypu, Idyll, and Mayor. All other words have Y as the third letter.

87. Historic.

88. Syrup does not belong to the group. The linked words are Cedar, Hedge, Medal, Sedan, and Wedge. All the words contain ED.

89. February.

90. Plant belongs to the group. The linked words are Burnt, Count, Event, Flint, and Giant. All the words end in NT.

91. Caffeine.

92. 5 ways

93. Unconstitutional.

94. 26 ways.

95. Disqualification.

96. 9 ways.

97. Characterization.

98. 22 ways.

99. Air-conditioning.

100. 14 ways.

101. Thanksgiving day.

102. 25 ways.

103. Acknowledgements.

104. Tango, Alien, Nines, Geese, and Onset.

105. Port.

106. 50. The alphabetical values of the letters are added together.

107. Ten.

108. Sat, Bacon, Anchors, and Each.

109. Yeast, Eager, Agave, Seven, and Trend.

110. Cot, Attic, Cushion, and Both.

111. Facet, Above, Coven, Event, and Tents.

112. Ripens and Sniper.

113. Smile, Mania, Inset, Liege, and Eater.

114. Arm, Enter, Mansion, and Arts.

115. Cheer does belong to the group. The associated words are Jetty, Comma, Annoy, Caddy, and Steel. Each have double letters.

116. Itself and Stifle.

117. Absence makes the heart grow fonder.

118. Eye.

119. Every man meets his Waterloo at last. Wendell Phillips.

120. Umpire and Impure.

121. Die my dear doctor thats the last thing I shall do. Lord Palmerston

122. Her.

123. One more such victory and we are lost. Pyrrhus.

124. End.

125. 6 ways.

126. 14. The alphabetical values of the first, third and fifth letters are added together.

127. Water.

128. Fire.

129. Flat.

130. Dance, Acorn, Nomad, Crave, and Ended.

131. Met, Amaze, Chamber, and Team.

132. Had, Blink, Academy, and Raid.

133. Ram.

134. Fantasy.

135. Writhes and Withers.

136. Macaroni.

137. Visor belongs to the group. The associated words are Vases, Denim, Widow, Focus, and Lotus. In each word the vowels appear in alphabetical order.

138. Pestered.

139. Globe does not belong to the group. The associated words are Hymns, Light, Ankle, Films, Index, and Pasta. Each word contains two letters next to each other which appear consecutively in the alphabet.

140. Deadline.

141. Widow belongs to the group. The associated words are Dread, Kiosk, Loyal, Arena, and Comic. Each word begins and ends with the same letter.

142. Teaspoon.

143. Cafes belongs to the group. The associated words are Babes, Games, Cakes, Paper, and Tales. Each have A

and E as their second and
fourth letter.

144. Gathered.

145. Comment is free but
facts are sacred. C.P. Scott.

146. Medalist.

147. Muscly and Clumsy.

148. Slate and Stale.

149. Long.

150. Jealousy.

151. Red.

152. Suitcase.

153. Boy.

154. Gardener.

155. Man.

156. Sun.

157. 1008. Each consonant is
worth 7 and each vowel 12.
The consonant total is multiplied by the vowel total.

158. Hollyhock, Buttercup,
and Dandelion.

159. S. To give Basic, Eased,
Haste (or Heats), and Music.

160. Butterfly, Centipede, and
Cockroach.

161. E. To give Agent, Bleak,
Enemy, and Query.

162. Decorator, Policeman,
and Architect.

163. V. To give Civic, Devil,
Haven, and Lever.

164. Coriander, Asparagus,
and Artichoke.

165. K. To give Joked, Maker, Taken, and Yokel.

166. Wolverine , Armadillo, and Porcupine.

167. 16 ways.

168. Psychotherapists.

169. Grace, Glace, Place, Peace.

170. Overcompensation.

171. Sort, Soot, Shot, Shop.

172. Responsibilities.

173. Prop, Poop, Pool, Poll, Pall.

174. 114. A is given the value 6, B is given 7 and so forth. The letter values in each word are added together.

175. Stare, Stars, Stays, Slays.

176. 57. The first and last letters are given the value of their position in the alphabet. These are then added together.

177. 5 ways.

178. The Name of the Rose.

179. Ability.

180. A Tale of Two Cities.

181. Badgers.

182. Star Trek the Movie.

183. Calypso.

184. George Washington.

185. Delight.

186. Winston Churchill.

187. Multimillionaire.

188. Extraterrestrial.

189. 11 ways.

190. Macaroon

191. 18 ways.

192. Ultimate.

193. 16 ways.

194. Horsefly.

195. 21 ways.

196. Puzzlers.

197. Glaze, Glare, Glary.

198. Radiance.

199. Intercontinental.

200. Instrumentalists

201. 10 ways.

202. Enthusiastically.

203. Crated and Carted.

204. Conservationists.

205. 8 ways.

206. Subconsciousness.

207. Read down the eighth column from the left, the first letter is on the third line.

208. The correct order is wolf, taxi, hair, ache.Fire is the thing which is hot.

209. Hand.

210. A B E H I.

211. The correct order is bird, book, vase, chef. The flower is rose.

212. Little Red Riding Hood.

213. Neigh, Snowy, Ready Thorn, Large.

214. Raiders of the Lost Ark.

215. Vincent Van Gogh, Leonardo da Vinci, Pablo Picasso, John Constable, Marc Chagall.

216. Creep, Alibi, Nails, Comic, Eagle, Rails. The signs of the zodiac are Cancer and Pisces.

217. No. The words in the box each begins with one of the vowels in their usual order.

218. Ski, Camp, Hail, Ocean, Olden, Lapel. The answer is school.

219. 1. Rain 2. Sun 3. Snow 4. Hail.

220. Tom Cruise.

221. The five words (Beach, Beans, Cease, Again, Drama) all have an A in the middle. Brass therefore fits.

222. Joust, Joist, Joint, Point, Paint, Pains. Clock, Cloak, Croak, Creak, Break, Bread.

223. Across. 1. Mast. 6. Orphan. 8. Pa. 9. Rear. 10. Ruler. 12. Drinks. 13. Do. 14. Hill. 16. Stag. 18. Gel. 19. Foal. 21. Door. 23. Corridor. Down. 1. Morning. 2. Are. 3. Spark. 4. Thrush. 5. Bandit. 7. Needle. 11. Roller. 15. Igloo. 16. Sap. 17. Also. 19. Far. 20. Add. 22. Or.

224. They are all composed of letters which, when laterally reversed, remain the same.

225. Rotate, Succulent, Dishwasher, Hostile, Nocturnal, Frontier, Lacerate, Unfurl, Misjudge, Quarterly

226. Portugal, Hungary, Romania, Germany, Greece.

227. Oliver Cromwell, Mahatma Gandhi, George Washington, William Cody, Michelle Pfeiffer, Julia Roberts, Robin Hood.

228. Electric, Longer, Ember, Cricket, Tablet, Rosemary, Oregano, Dawdle, Eternal. The word is electrode.

229. Bugle, Attack, Tank, Tactics, Lieutenant, Enemy. The word is battle.

230. Cinderella.

231. Iceland.

232. Swimming, Archery, Football, Athletics, Riding, Ice skating. The word is Safari.

233. Blackguard, Blueberry, Blueprint, Blackbeard, Greenhouse

234. Consonants are worth 4, vowels 2, therefore Washington DC is 42 miles away.

235. Staple, Pastel, Palest, Plates, Pleats, Petals.

236. Bob, Bobs, Bobsleigh, Bosh, Bole, Boles, Boil, Boils, Bog, Bogs, Bogie, Bogies, Blob, Blobs, Beg, Begs, Bib, Bibs, Bible, Bibles, Bile, Bilge, Big, Oblige, Obliges, Obeli, Oil, Oils Ogle, Ogles, Ohs, Sob, Sol, Sole, Soli, Soil, Soh, Slob, Sloe, Slog, Sleigh, Silo, Sigh, Shoe, She, Lob, Lobbies, Lobs, Lobe, Lobes, Lose, Log, Logs, Loge, Loges, Lei, Leis, Leg, Legs, Lib, Lie, Lies, Ebb, Ebbs, Ego, Egos, Isle, Gob, Gobs, Gobble, Gobbles, Goch, Goes, Glob, Globs, Globe, Globes, Glib, Gel, Gels, Gib, Gibboxe, Gibs, Gibe, Gibes, Hob, Hobble, Hobbles, Hobbies, Hobs, Hose, Hole, Holes, Holies, Hoe, Hoes,

Hog, Hogs, His, Hie, Hies.

237. 1. Mansfield Park
– Jane Austen. 2. Hard Times
– Charles Dickens. 3. Romeo
and Juliet – William
Shakespeare. 4. Tess of the
d'Urbervilles – Thomas Hardy.

238. Green Brian (Big Ben,
Old Glory, Union Jack, Blue
Beard, Stormin' Norman).

239. Palace, Cottage,
ungalow, Castle, Monastery.
Cedar, Redwood, Hickory,
Maple, Hornbeam.

240. Bugs, (all curved letters
– no straight lines).

241.

242. Arm, Head, Leg, Foot.

243. Sonic the Hedgehog.

244.

245. Abdomen, Bureaucrat,
Diversion, Flabbergast,
Indicate, Longitude,
Newspaper, Romantic,
Sustenance, Volunteer.

246. All the words (Ready,
Anything, Yellow, Analysis,
Acolyte) contain Y. Heady
fits.

247. Noiseless Lionesses.

248. Acrobatic.

249. Indigo, Number, Treaty, Race, India, Glue, Umbrella, Elephant.
The word is intrigue.

250.

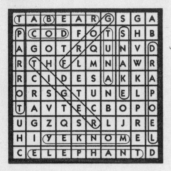

251. Consonants are worth 7, vowels 8. Therefore Beijing is 53 miles away.

252. The correct order is omen, pole, fork, knee.
The word is moon.

253. The Wizard of Oz. Close Encounters of the Third Kind. Pollyanna. Back to the Future. National Velvet.,Batman Returns. Beauty and the Beast. Honey I Shrunk the Kids. The Sound of Music. Jurassic Park.

254. A.

255. Only one, of course. We did tell you it was a trick!

256. E.

257. The five words (Anteater, Eagles, Ahead, Azalea, Nausea) all have EA in them.Confidence won't fit.

258. Fast, Area, Sets, Task.

259. 1. Phantom of the Opera. 2. Carousel. 3.Evita. 4.Starlight Express. 5.The Sound of Music. 6.Les Miserables. 7.Chess. 8.Miss Saigon. 9.Rocky Horror Show. 10.Cats.

260. Rumplestiltskin.

261. Cormorant, Crow, Cuckoo, Chaffinch, Canary.

262. The correct order is shop, away need, down. Sand is found on the beach.

263. Back.

264. Catapult.
(All the words include the name of an animal.)

265. Modicum, Cadmium, Academic, Dummied, Acceded.

266.

267. United States of America.

268. 1. Mar, Ram, Arm.
2. Art, Tar, Rat. 3. Spar, Pars, Raps, Rasp. 4. Miles, Slime, Smile, Limes.

269. The five words (Average, Ear, Introduction, Onomatopoeia, Uncle) all begin with vowels.
Ability fits.

270. Bulldog, Dogfish.

271. Mother Goose.

272. Winona Ryder.

273. Pa, Pan, Pane, Panel.

274. See next page. Theme is the word that appears twice.

275. John Lennon, Helena Bonham-Carter, Napoleon Bonaparte, Elizabeth Taylor, Neil Armstrong, Albert Einstein, Richard Gere.

276. California, Idaho, Nebraska, Hawaii, Alaska.

277. Consonants are worth 3, vowels 12. Therefore Yale should be 30 miles away.

278. Andre Agassi.

279. Apple, Norman, Opera, Night, Yellow, Mark, Opium, Ugly, Sea. The word is anonymous.

274.

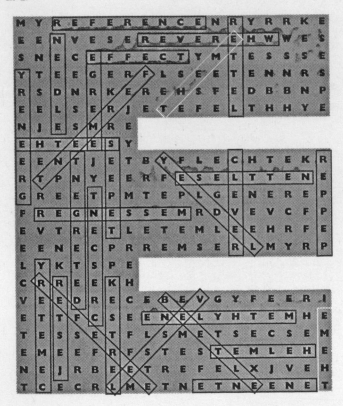

NOTES

NOTES

NOTES

NOTES

NOTES

NOTES

NOTES

NOTES

NOTES

NOTES

NOTES

NOTES

NOTES

NOTES

NOTES

NOTES